Foundation Db2 and Python

Access Db2 with Module-Based API Examples Using Python

W. David Ashley

Apress®

Foundation Db2 and Python

W. David Ashley
Austin, TX, USA

ISBN-13 (pbk): 978-1-4842-6941-1
https://doi.org/10.1007/978-1-4842-6942-8

ISBN-13 (electronic): 978-1-4842-6942-8

Managing Director, Apress Media LLC: Welmoed Spahr
Acquisitions Editor: Celestin Suresh John
Development Editor: James Markham
Coordinating Editor: Divya Modi

Cover designed by eStudioCalamar

Cover image designed by Pixabay

Distributed to the book trade worldwide by Springer Science+Business Media New York, 1 New York Plaza, Suite 4600, New York, NY 10004-1562, USA. Phone 1-800-SPRINGER, fax (201) 348-4505, e-mail orders-ny@ springer-sbm.com, or visit www.springeronline.com. Apress Media, LLC is a California LLC and the sole member (owner) is Springer Science + Business Media Finance Inc (SSBM Finance Inc). SSBM Finance Inc is a **Delaware** corporation.

For information on translations, please e-mail booktranslations@springernature.com; for reprint, paperback, or audio rights, please e-mail bookpermissions@springernature.com.

Apress titles may be purchased in bulk for academic, corporate, or promotional use. eBook versions and licenses are also available for most titles. For more information, reference our Print and eBook Bulk Sales web page at http://www.apress.com/bulk-sales.

Any source code or other supplementary material referenced by the author in this book is available to readers on GitHub via the book's product page, located at www.apress.com/978-1-4842-6941-1. For more detailed information, please visit http://www.apress.com/source-code.

Printed on acid-free paper

This book is dedicated to teachers everywhere, but especially all those who had me as a student.

Table of Contents

About the Author

W. David Ashley is a technical writer for Skillsoft where he specializes in open source, particularly Linux. As a member of the Linux Fedora documentation team, he recently led the Libvirt project documentation and wrote the Python programs included with it. He has developed in 20 different programming languages during his 30 years as a software developer and IT consultant, including more than 18 years at IBM and 12 years with American Airlines.

About the Technical Reviewer

Sourav Bhattacharjee is a senior technical member for Oracle Cloud Infrastructure. As part of IBM Watson Health Lab, he has developed many scalable systems, published a few research papers, and applied some patents to USPTO. He has an ample amount of hands-on experience in Python, Java, machine learning, and many database systems. He earned his master's degree from the Indian Institute of Technology, Kharagpur, India.

CHAPTER 1

Introduction to Db2

Welcome to this introduction to Db2. Since you are here, you are likely looking for a place to get started with Db2. Our hope is that this book will be that first step you are looking for. This book is meant to be an introduction to the Db2 environment and to the Python interface. The first half of the book will cover Db2 at a level that should be of interest to both administrators and programmers. It will cover many aspects of Db2 that you will make use of in either of the two roles. The last half of the book will concentrate on using the Python programming language to interface to Db2. While mainly oriented to programmers, administrators will find it useful as well for some of their everyday tasks.

Db2 has a long history and is the first relational database implementation. It was first proposed by Edgar Frank "Ted" Codd in a paper titled "A Relational Model of Data for Large Shared Data Banks" in 1969 while working at the IBM's San Jose Research Laboratory in California. In the next four years, IBM researchers worked to create a system based on the principles described in Codd's paper (called System R). During this time, it became obvious that a new language was needed to interact with the new system. Codd wrote a new paper "A Data Base Sublanguage Founded on Relational Calculus," which became the basis for the new language called DSL/Alpha. This quickly went through some name changes but eventually ended up being called SQL, short for Structured Query Language.

Eventually there was an effort in the 1970s to port DSL/Alpha to the 370 mainframe environment. It was renamed to Database 2 in 1982. The next year it was made available to the public with another name change, DB2. This was a limited release but was highly regarded by the customers that evaluated it. The customers actually pushed IBM to deliver DB2 to a wider set of customers. IBM was somewhat reluctant because they were trying to hold on to their IMS/DB market share. But eventually the customers won out, and DB2 began to spread to other platforms including OS/2, AIX/RS6000, and Windows.

© W. David Ashley 2021
W. D. Ashley, *Foundation Db2 and Python*, https://doi.org/10.1007/978-1-4842-6942-8_1

Over the next two decades, the product went through a number of name changes and several platform code bases. Recently with the release of version 11.1, IBM rebranded the entire product line and brought the code bases into a small number of code bases. The following set of products are now the standard offerings:

- Db2 (formerly DB2 LUW)

- Db2 for z/OS (formerly DB2 for z/OS)

- Db2 Hosted (formerly DB2 on Cloud)

- Db2 on Cloud (formerly dashDB for Transactions)

- Db2 Event Store (a new in-memory database for event-driven transaction processing)

- Db2 Warehouse on Cloud (formerly dashDB)

- Db2 Warehouse (formerly dashDB Local)

- IBM Integrated Analytics System (a new system platform that combines analytic performance and functionality of the IBM PureData System with IBM Netezza)

The code bases for today's Db2 offerings share a common code base that makes porting the code to another hardware/software platform a relatively easy process. The SQL code base has been standardized so that it is the same across all platforms, making moving to another platform an easy task from a programming perspective.

There is also a current movement in programming applications with embedded SQL. These types of applications are very hard to port from one platform to another without major code modifications. Instead, IBM is moving (where possible) to an API that can be called to process SQL statements and make use of programming language variables for values to be added to the SQL statement. This is the methodology used for Python that we will explore later in this book.

In the past, Db2 was considered to be too large for most applications. But as personal computers have become a lot more powerful and then databases used by even a small number of people have become extremely large, Db2 has become more attractive in the management of this data. Also, the pricing model of Db2 on these platforms has become more competitive. So if you need the performance and the ability to manage large amounts of data, Db2 can be a very attractive product.

What Is a Relational Database?

A relational database is actually hard to define because no relational database system in today's market actually implements E. F. Codd's 12 rules defining the relational model. Instead, commercial relational databases implement only about seven to nine of those rules. This is enough to make their products commercially useful without the burden of implementing the other rules. In fact, the other rules would not be useful to most database users, so it is questionable whether or not they will ever be implemented in a commercial product. In fact, most commercial database vendors actually extend the relational model by adding entities that are not really tables, such as BLOBs (which we will discuss later).

The Relational Model

Roughly, relational databases implement the concept of entities expressed as rows and columns. A customer records table would have a single row representing a single customer. The columns (or tuples) of the table would contain attributes of that customer. Each column would contain a single attribute and would have a defined data type for restricting the type of information it can contain. A typical customer address table might be implemented as shown in Table 1-1.

Table 1-1. *Sample Customer Table*

CUSTNO	FNAME	LNAME	STREET	STATE	ZIP
000000001	Bugs	Bunny	1201 Looney Lane	CA	77777
000000002	Marvin	Martian	2342 Mars Avenue	MA	30143
000000003	Daffy	Duck	5462 Termite Terrace	CA	77745
000000004	Elmer	Fudd	23 Hunter Cove	CA	77732

This table is a good example because it shows the kind of relationships that can be expressed in a relational database. The CUSTNO column holds a unique customer number for each customer (or row). The column is the primary key for this table. The FNAME and LNAME identify the first and last names of the customer. The STREET is the address to be used for billing the customer. The STATE column is the U.S. state the address is located. The ZIP column identifies the mailing zip code.

Domains

Domains (or attributes) limit the data in a column to a particular type. For instance, the data might be an integer of a particular type, a monetary value, a character string of fixed or variable length, a date or time value, or some other domain that has been defined.

Keys and Indexes

The STATE column in Table 1-1 is a foreign key – that is, a primary key in another table. A rule can be set up so that when you add a new row to the customer table, the system checks that the value in your proposed STATE field is a valid entry in the state table. If it is not, the record will not be inserted, and an error will be generated. Keys are also known as indexes. When you create a primary key in a table, a special index table is created to hold valid keys. This table is like any other table in the system; it can be queried, added to, and deleted from. Thus, all the valid keys can be inserted into and maintained in the table, and it can be maintained just like any other table. Only the special rules make the index table special.

Relationships

All of this shows just some of the kinds of relationships that can be created (or derived) to properly maintain a set of tables. There are probably other kinds of customer tables that could be created like a table to maintain customer credit ratings, a customer shipping address table, a customer contacts table, etc. All of these are specialized entities that have relationships with the other customer tables. This is what a relational database is all about. The idea is to express a relationship with data organized so the data is only stored where needed and hopefully only one time.

Relationships allow the user to create customized reports that can express custom views of the data from the database. At first glance these reports may look like they have no relation to the data contained in the database, but they can give insights to the data not easily possible by other means.

Transactions

Another aspect of relational databases is support for transactions. This means providing a locking mechanism that can allow data to be modified while others are reading the data or modifying other data at the same time. This is known as the ACID test, which is an acronym for the following tests:

- Atomicity defines all the elements that make up a complete database transaction. This might make up one or more SQL statements.

- Consistency defines the rules for maintaining data points in the correct state after a transaction. This is usually done through an SQL statement such as COMMIT or ROLLBACK.

- Isolation keeps the effect of a transaction invisible to others until it is committed, to avoid confusion. This refers to the ability of the database to keep multiple changes to a database from corrupting the integrity of the database.

- Durability ensures that data changes become permanent once the transaction is committed. This is done by ensuring that writes are made to all modified tables prior to committing the transaction.

Stored Procedures

A relational database typically implements stored procedures. These are programs stored in the database to implement special processing under several circumstances. These procedures usually involve business logic that needs to be implemented the same across all the database users. In many cases, only the stored procedure has the proper permissions to modify, insert, delete, or access the data being manipulated. This prevents users from making modifications to the data if they do not have the correct permissions.

Constraints

Another property of relational databases are constraints. These make it possible to further restrict an attribute. For instance, a column might be defined as an integer. But the range of numbers might actually need to be constrained to a particular range. This is what a constraint provides.

Constraints can come in many forms and are used for a number of purposes. They are stored within the database and used when adding or modifying data.

Normalization

Normalization is another attribute of a relational database. This design process reduces the number of nonatomic values and the duplication of data throughout the database, thus preventing anomalies and loss of integrity. The process is known as normalization.

The process of normalization is performed by the administrator, usually during the creation of the database. Users are not usually involved in this activity.

SQL

Within the first few years of creating the first relational database, it became very obvious that something was needed to actually manipulate the data in a relational database. The language was invented at IBM by Donald D. Chamberlin and Raymond F. Boyce in the early 1970s. It was originally known as SEQUEL, but that name was trademarked and it was changed to Structured Query Language (SQL). SQL was later standardized by ANSI, but each relational database product extended it as needed to conform to their product or hardware platform.

SQL is divided into four categories of statements:

- Data Definition Language (DDL)

- Data Query Language (DQL)

- Data Control Language (DCL)

- Data Manipulation Language (DML)

Most SQL books spend most of their resources on the DML part of SQL, but the other parts are just as important, especially to the database administrator.

Data Definition Language (DDL)

The Data Definition Language subset consists of the CREATE, DROP, ALTER, and TRUNCATE statements. These statements manipulate (or reorganize) the data in the database.

The CREATE statement creates new entities in the database. This can include tables, indexes, views, and procedures. Many database systems include character sets, collations, transactions, and assertions as well.

The DROP statement removes entities from the database. These include all the entities that can be created with the CREATE statement. Some databases include the users as an entity that can be dropped.

The ALTER statement can alter an existing entity, such as adding a new column to a table.

The TRUNCATE statement removes all data from a table or index. It is much faster than the DELETE SQL statement.

Data Query Language (DQL)

The Data Query Language subset consists of only the SELECT statement. This is used for all queries of information in the database. The syntax of the SELECT statement will be covered later in Chapter 7.

Data Control Language (DCL)

The Data Control Language subset consists of the GRANT and REVOKE statements. These statements grant and revoke privileges to and from users of the database. The database system specifies the type of privileges that a user can be granted. Some database systems, such as SQLite, depend on the operating system's privilege mechanism and thus do not support the GRANT and REVOKE statements.

Data Manipulation Language (DML)

The Data Manipulation Language subset consists of the INSERT, UPDATE, and DELETE statements. Some systems also include the SELECT statement in this subset, but since SELECT does not make changes to the data, this would seem an odd place to place the SELECT statement.

The INSERT statement adds new rows into a table. This new data may also automatically alter the content of a view of the table data.

The UPDATE statement alters one or more rows in an existing table (and any view dependent on the table). The statement does not add new rows to a table, it only alters existing data.

The DELETE statement removes rows from a table (and any view dependent on the table).

The ibm_db Project

The ibm_db project was started sometime in 2007 with the first code commits to GitHub on February 9, 2008. The project was a joint effort between IBM and the Python community to create a programming interface to Db2 and Informix from Python. Informix had been purchased by IBM around this same time, and this was part of the project to integrate Informix into the Db2 line of products. Since then the project has undergone steady progress with some recent major fixes.

By establishing the project on GitHub, it was thought that with community support the project would not only improve with time but would benefit from community participation. This has proven to be the case with many community volunteers contributing to the project throughout the project lifetime.

Over time, the ibm_db_dbi module was added to the project, and new projects were introduced based on the ibm_db module to support other Python projects. These projects include ibm_db_django, ibm_db_alembic, and ibm_db_sa.

For more information, see Chapter 8.

Summary

This chapter has presented some of the basic concepts that make up a relational database and the SQL that supports it. This information is common to almost all relational databases.

CHAPTER 2

Installing Db2

This chapter covers installing Db2 on Linux and Windows. Both environments use the same installer to perform installation and creation of userids and permissions. The installation process is pretty easy and straightforward, but there are a number of questions you might have before you start the installation that are not answered by the install program. We will try to cover those questions as we come to them.

My Development Environment

My development environment is not your typical Windows home system. It consists of two Linux servers, one Windows client, and two Linux client workstations. The Linux servers are not typical workstations but actual dedicated servers that are usually used in small business settings. I will try to describe each system so you have some idea of what my environment is like.

The first system is a Lenovo ThinkSystem ST250 server with four 2 TB drives installed. It has 32 GB of memory and a six-core Xeon CPU. This is my main server and hosts all my files. It is visible to the Internet through my firewall via the Apache Web Server. The operating system is Fedora 32. It is also hosting my Windows files via Samba as well as hosting a number of Virtual Machines (VMs) via libvirt. This is the system that hosts my main Db2 databases.

The second system is Lenovo ThinkStation P320 with 256 GB of SSD and a 1 TB drive with 32 GB of memory and a six-core/six-thread Xeon CPU. This is my development server and actually changes configuration about twice a year. It currently runs CentOS Linux 8.2. This machine also hosts my test Db2 environment.

The third machine is my Windows 10 workstation. It is connected to the first Linux system via a shared drive (Samba) on the server. This is where I do most of my writing as well as Windows development and testing.

9

© W. David Ashley 2021
W. D. Ashley, *Foundation Db2 and Python*, https://doi.org/10.1007/978-1-4842-6942-8_2

The fourth system is a Lenovo ThinkCentre M920 with 256 GB of SSD and a 1 TB drive with 16 GB of memory. It has an i7 CPU. This is my development workstation where I test all my Linux development and remote access to servers. The operating system is Fedora 32.

The fifth system is a Lenovo ThinkPad T580 with 256 GB of SSD, 16 GB of memory, and an i7 CPU. It runs Fedora 32 and usually serves as my travel machine but also as an auxiliary test device.

Installation Prerequisites

Before you even start the Db2 install program, there are a number of prerequisites that need to be met before you can successfully install everything. Our install environment for this book is CentOS 8.2. The prerequisites for this OS should be the same for RHEL 8.2, but may be different for other Linux environments. Windows environments have their own prerequisites, but they are similar to the Linux prerequisites.

The first thing we need is the Db2 install program and support files. To get the free version of Db2, just go to

```
www.ibm.com/account/reg/us-en/signup?formid=urx-33669
```

This gets you to the account registration page. You can either log in with an existing userid or create a new one. After you are logged in, the website will present you a preferences page. Select your preferences and select the Continue button. On the next web page, select the download you need. Unless you need them, just ignore the pureScale support downloads. Once the download is complete, move the downloaded file to a safe location and then unzip or untar it. This will create a new subdirectory in the current directory with the install files exploded inside.

Caution!   Do not move the downloaded file to the directory you intend to place databases. You will have a mess of files on your hands when you create your first database.

At the time this book was written, the version of Db2 that was available was version 11.5.4. Older free versions of Db2 are not made available when IBM introduces a new version.

Now that you have your evaluation version of Db2, you are probably wondering what its limitations are. The evaluation version does not ever expire. It has no limitation on the number of databases. The one and only limitation is the total size of all databases, currently limited to 100 GB. This is more than enough space to perform your own evaluation of the software unless you are trying to test a very large system. If that is your plan, IBM will be more than glad to help with a production version of Db2 and even some engineers.

At this point, we are now ready to find out what our prerequisites are. To do this, simply run the install program. This program is located in the untarred subdirectory we previously created. The expanded directory is named server_dec. To run the install program, just run the following commands:

```
$ cd server_dec
$ ./db2setup
```

If prerequisites are needed by Db2, the install program will list them and then exit. Be sure to read everything output by the install program. On our CentOS 8.2 system, it listed two prerequisites:

- libpam.so*   (32-bit)

- libstdc++.so.6   (32-bit)

"Wait. Why does Db2 need 32-bit libraries?" you ask. Db2 is a collection of a bunch of products, some of which have not changed in a decade or more. Rather than possibly introducing new bugs into the system, IBM has chosen to keep the older version of some of these products. Thus, these prerequisite libraries are needed to support those products.

Use your system's software installer to install the prerequisite packages. For Linux, this will be either the dnf or yum programs for RPM-based packages. Once you have the prerequisites installed, you are ready to proceed to really installing Db2. But before we do that, we need to do a little planning.

Planning the Db2 Install

Before we get to the install, we need to understand what the result of the install will be so we can plan ahead and avoid surprises afterward. There are two major points to cover in this area.

The first result of the install is that you will have two new userids created on the target machine. The default names of these IDs are db2inst1 and db2fenc1. The db2inst1 ID will have some files stored in its home directory, and you need to make sure there is enough space to accommodate them. There are a limited number of files, but you should make sure you are prepared for them. The db2fenc1 ID only has a very limited number of files stored in its home directory.

The second result is not really a result of the install. It is more a default that is set as a result of the install. This item is the location where databases will be installed. The default location for databases is in the db2inst1 home directory! THIS IS NOT WHERE YOU WANT TO STORE DATABASES! You are probably going to store them on a different drive/location. We will discuss this point again after we cover the install process and before we create the sample database.

There are also a few minor points that are a result of the install, but we will cover those as we get to them.

Installing Db2

We are now ready to install Db2. This process must be done by the root (on Linux) or admin (on Windows) user, so start by becoming the root/admin user. On Windows you will need to log out and log back in as the admin user. On Linux just perform the following command:

```
$ su - root
```

After this you need to change to the directory where you placed the expanded files of the Db2 download package. Then run the db2setup install package:

```
$ cd server_dec
$ ./db2setup
```

If you have installed all the prerequisites, this should show you the Welcome page (Figure 2-1).

Figure 2-1. *Db2 Install Welcome Page*

After you click the *New Install* button, the next window appears to allow you to select a product to install (Figure 2-2).

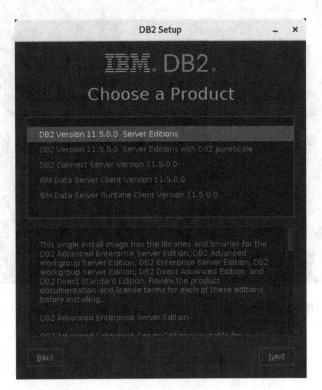

Figure 2-2. *Db2 Install Choose a Product Page*

This page has a number of products that you can select. The first product is *Db2 Server*, and this is the product we will install. The second product is *Db2 with pureScale*, which we did not download. The third product is *Db2 Connect Server*, which is used for distributed databases. The fourth product is *Db2 Connect Client*, which is used for building compiled code that includes SQL statements. The last product is *Db2 Runtime Client*, which is used for running compiled code from the *Db2 Connect Client* version.

At this point you should select the top item in the list, *Db2 Server Editions*. The version number may be different if you downloaded a newer version of Db2. The other selections are not important at this point in time. After clicking the *Next* button, the next page will appear.

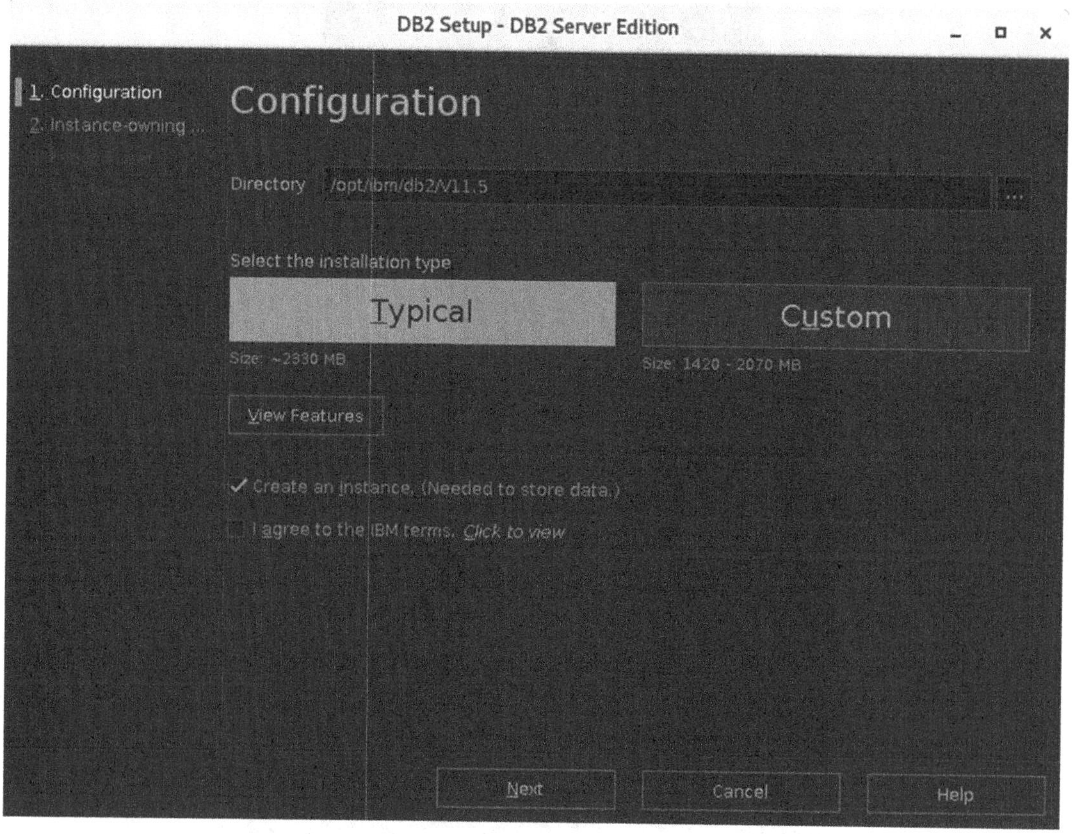

Figure 2-3. *Db2 Install Configuration Page*

The Configuration page allows you to select either a *Typical* or a *Custom* install. At this point, select a *Typical* install. You must also check the box to agree to the IBM terms before you proceed. When finished, click the *Next* button and the next page shown in Figure 2-4 will appear.

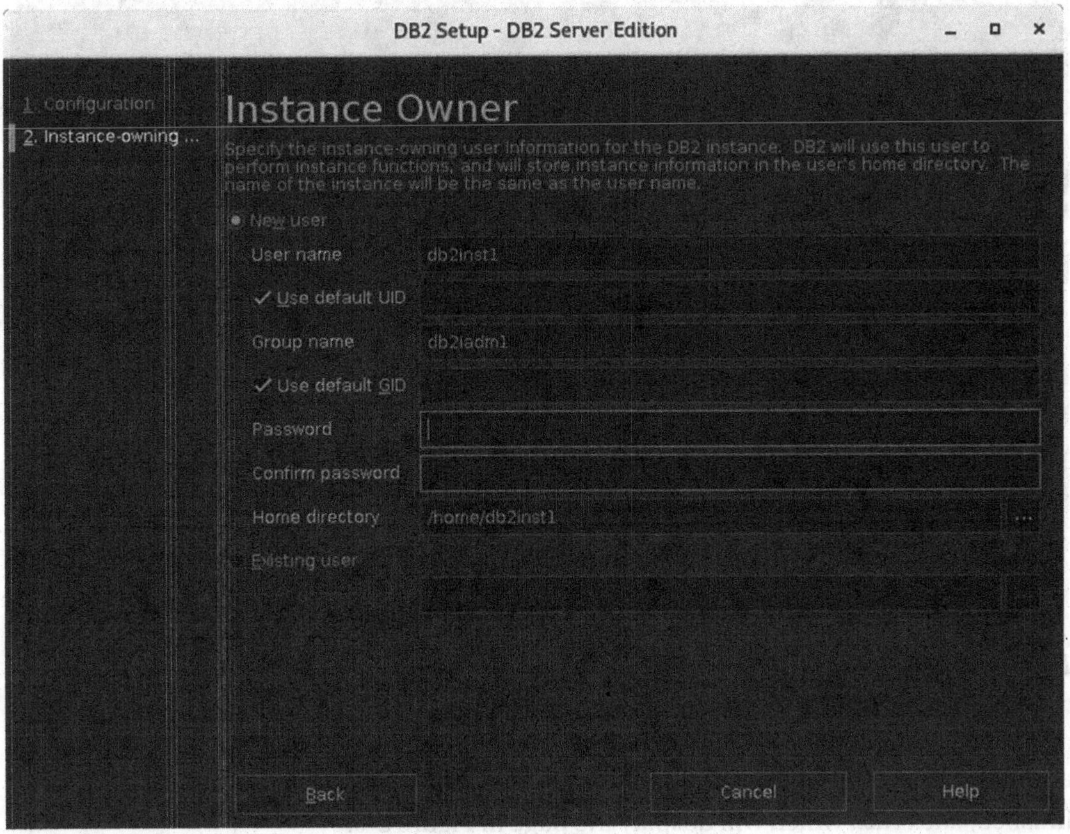

Figure 2-4. *Db2 Install Instance Owner Page*

You can check out the *Custom* install option for some items you may want to change. Most users just perform a *Typical* install.

The Instance Owner page allows you to create the account that will own the first instance of Db2 and the group name of the new user. Just leave the db2inst1 information as it appears and then enter the password and confirmation for the new account. This is the account that will have new files installed in its home directory. When you have entered in the new password and confirmed it for the account, click *Next* and the page shown in Figure 2-5 will be displayed.

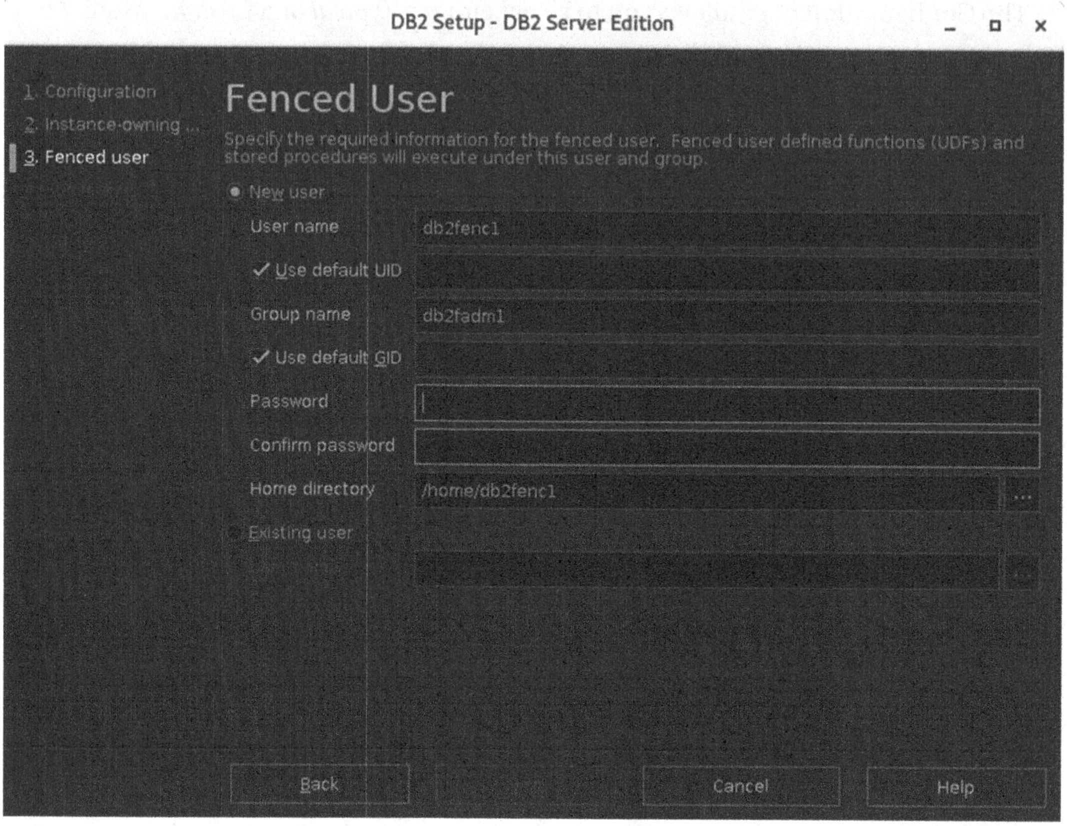

Figure 2-5. *Db2 Install Fenced User Page*

The db2fenc1 user will run user-defined functions and stored procedures outside the address space of the Db2 database. Enter the db2fenc1 password and confirm it. When finished, click *Next* which will dosplay the page in Figure 2-6.

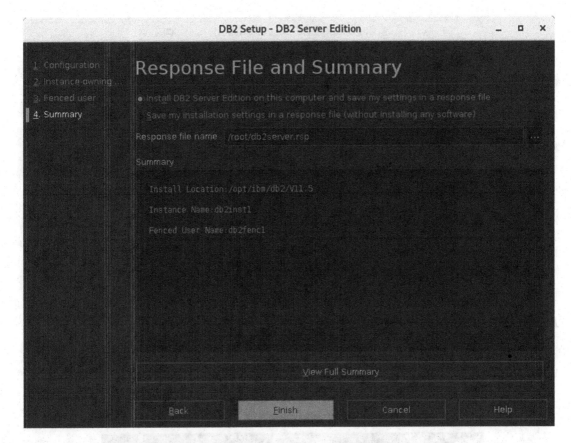

Figure 2-6. *Db2 Install Response File and Summary Page*

The next page is the Response File and Summary page. The response file is a part of the installation set of files, so it does not have to be created. Click the *Finish* button to start the install of Db2 as shown in Figure 2-7.

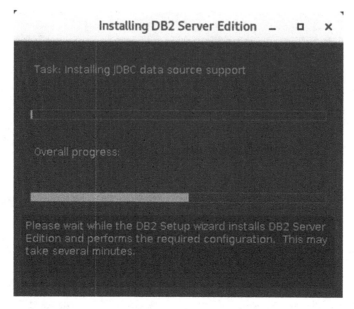

Figure 2-7. *Db2 Install Progress Page*

The two status bars keep track of the progress of the installation of all components. When finished, you will automatically be taken to next page (Figure 2-8).

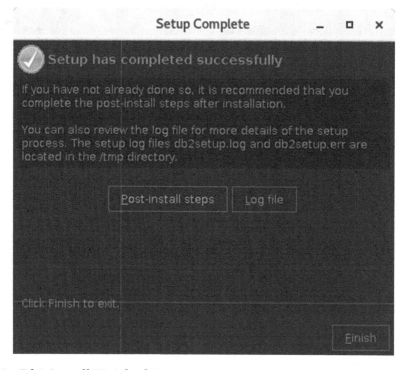

Figure 2-8. *Db2 Install Finished Page*

When the installation is complete, this is the page that *w*ill be shown. You can choose to review the post-install steps, review the log file, or just click the *Finish* button to exit the install.

At this point, the Db2 installation steps are complete, and we are ready to look at the post-install tasks that will need to be considered.

Note   With Ubuntu Linux, the Db2 instance owner and fenced user that are created by the Db2 install are assigned the Dash shell by default. This can cause scripts that begin with the line *#!/bin/bash* to stop working. If you want to use Bash as the default shell when you log into either of these users, execute the command **csh -s /bin/bash username** (where **username** is the name of the Db2 instance owner or fenced user) before doing anything else.

Db2 Post-install Tasks

There are a few tasks that need to be performed after the Db2 install has completed:

1. Try to log into the db2fenc1 userid using the password you set from the db2setup command. Correct any problems you may find.

2. Try to log into the db2inst1 userid using the password you set from the db2setup command. Correct any problems you may find. You should note the location of the sqllib directory and its contents as you may need to become familiar with them. This may or may not be a link to another location.

3. If you do not want databases stored in the db2inst1 directory tree, then now is the time to change that location. Log in as the db2inst1 userid and run the following command:

   ```
   $ db2 update dbm cfg using dftdbpath /your/db/path
   ```

This will update the path in the Db2 configuration so that all databases belonging to db2inst1 will be stored in the new location.

At this point, we are now finished with our post-install tasks, and we are ready to proceed to installing the sample database.

Installing the Db2 Sample Database

Db2 comes with a default database named sample. This database, although small, is comprehensive enough to show how a database should be constructed and is useful for demonstrating an array of possible SQL commands. This book uses the sample database extensively for demonstrating Db2 concepts, SQL usage, and Python programming examples.

To install the sample database, follow these steps.

Log into the db2inst1 userid:

```
$ su - db2inst1
```

The Db2 database instance needs to be started, so that is our next step:

```
$ db2start
```

Now we can actually install the sample database. This command will take a few minutes, so be patient:

```
$ db2sampl -force -sql
```

The -force option ensures that if the database is already installed, it will be overlaid with the default content. The -sql option tells Db2 not to install the XML data into the database.

Now we can connect to the database and test it:

```
$ db2 connect to sample
```

If successful, you should see some output that looks something like this:

```
  Database Connection Information

 Database server        = DB2/LINUXX8664 11.5.0.0
 SQL authorization ID   = DB2INST1
 Local database alias   = SAMPLE
```

Now we can run a test SQL command to query the database:

```
$ db2 "select * from department"
```

Important   Be sure to include quotes around the text that follows **db2**. If the quotes are omitted, the operating system will try to process the command incorrectly, and an error will result.

You should see a total of 14 records displayed if everything works as expected. We can now terminate our connection to the database with the following command:

```
$ db2 connect reset
```

If successful, our connection to the database is now terminated.

Summary

This chapter has presented the steps to installing and verifying the installation of Db2. Be sure to read the Caution, Note, and Important sections presented in the chapter as they have valuable information for some operating systems.

CHAPTER 3

Db2 Management

The management of Db2 is not an easy affair. It is not like any open source relational database. It is a little like Oracle, but there are differences. This is because Db2 for Linux, Unix, and Windows is a lot like maintaining a mainframe database, just on a smaller and easier scale. While there are many tools to help manage the Db2 environment contained in the product itself, the key to proper management is understanding the architecture of the product and how it manages hardware resources. Without this knowledge, it is easy to get into trouble and overextend the hardware of the machine. With proper management, a single piece of hardware can manage either a few large databases or many smaller ones without stretching the resources on the machine too far.

This chapter will give you enough knowledge so that you can set up the Db2 environment properly without overburdening you with facts that have few, if any, consequences.

Db2 Instances

Instances are the top-level architectural structure in Db2. When you installed Db2, you created the first Db2 Instance, which had the default name of db2inst1. This is also the Instance that holds the sample database we installed in the previous chapter.

Any number of databases can be installed in an Instance. But it is possible to overload an Instance and cause performance problems. This is because Db2 sets aside a fixed number of processes and threads for each Instance, and it does not dynamically add or remove resources during the active lifetime of an Instance. You must stop the instance, adjust the number of resources, and then restart the Instance. Of course, the databases owned by the Instance will have to be stopped and restarted as well. That is the key: stopping and starting an Instance can have impacts on availability and the contained databases. If you are continually stopping and restarting Instances, your users will not be very happy with your management skills.

23

© W. David Ashley 2021
W. D. Ashley, *Foundation Db2 and Python*, https://doi.org/10.1007/978-1-4842-6942-8_3

Instances are easy to describe, but harder to justify. You have to know some history to be able to properly understand where they came from as well as why they even exist. Instances were first introduced just after the year 2000. Their justification came as the databases on multi-drive machines started to become very large. They were so large and had so many users that the network interface became a bottleneck in processing database requests. It seems that the machines now far outpaced the network in being able to handle database requests. Db2 had plenty of idle time while it waited on the network interface to process the next request. This was in the days when the fastest common networks were only 10 MB capacity. What was needed was a way to divide the databases among multiple network ports. Thus, instances were born.

Instances were not only given their own network port, they were also given their own processes, threads, and semaphores. Thus, if a database crashed for any reason, it would only disrupt the databases within the containing Instance. The other Instances and databases would continue to run normally while the database administrator dealt with the downed Instance.

Instances can be used in many ways by the database administrator, but the most common use is to prevent network port congestion. The second most common use is to separate sets of databases from each other for security purposes. Since each Instance has its own set of administrators and users, this helps to enforce security between Instances.

One other attribute of an instance is that it has no physical presence on your disk system, or at least not much of one. It is very hard to point to a place in the disk system and say, "This is where an instance resides." There are a few files created with the instance, but these do not describe where the instance is. You should just think of it as a logical entity and not a physical one.

There is a set of commands that administrators can use to manage instances. The following are some example Db2 commands that manage Instances.

Note   All the commands used in this chapter can be run in one of two ways. They can be run by logging into the db2inst1 user, or they can be run by using the sudo db2inst1 prefix to the command.

---

db2ilist

This command lists all the Instances that are available on a system:

```
db2ilist
```

Output:

```
db2inst1
db2inst2
db2inst3
```

Instance Environment Commands

These commands are useful to work with arrangement of instances in the Db2 CLI.

The following command obtains the current instance:

```
db2 get instance
```

Output:

```
The current database manager instance is : db2inst1
```

To start or stop the database manager of an instance on Db2 UDB, the following command is executed for the current instance:

```
set db2instance=db2inst1
```

Using this command, you can start an Instance. Before this, you need to run "set instance":

```
db2start
```

Output:

```
SQL1063N DB2START processing was successful
```

This command is used to stop the current Instance:

```
db2stop
```

Output:

```
SQL1064N DB2STOP processing was successful.
```

Creating an Instance

Let us see how to create a new Instance.

If you want to create a new Instance, you need to log in with root. An Instance ID is not a root ID or a root name.

Here are the steps to create a new Instance:

Step 1: Create an operating system user for an Instance.

```
useradd -u <ID> -g <group name> -m -d <user location> <user name> -p <password>
```

Example:

```
useradd -u 1000 -g db2iadm1 -m -d /home/db2inst2 db2inst2 -p db2inst2
```

Step 2: Go to the Db2 Instance directory as a root user to create a new Instance. Location:

```
cd /opt/ibm/db2/v10.1/instance
```

Step 3: Create an instance using the following syntax.

```
./db2icrt -s ese -u <inst id> <instance name>
```

Example:

```
./db2icrt -s ese -u db2inst2 db2inst2
```

Output:

```
DBI1446I The db2icrt command is running, please wait.
  ....
  .....
DBI1070I Program db2icrt completed successfully.
```

Arranging a Communication Port and Host for an Instance

Edit the /etc/services file and add the port number. In the following syntax, "inst_name" indicates the Instance name, and "inst_port" indicates the port number of the Instance:

```
db2c_<inst name> <inst_port>/tcp
```

Example:

```
sudo - db2c_db2inst2 50001/tcp
```

Syntax 1: Update configuration with the service name. In the following syntax, "svcename" indicates the Instance service name, and "inst_name" indicates the Instance name.

```
db2 update database manager configuration using svcename db2c_&<inst_name>
```

Example 1: Updating DBM configuration with variable svcename with value "db2c_db2inst2" for Instance "db2inst2"

```
db2 update database manager configuration using svcename db2c_db2inst2
```

Output,:

```
DB20000I The UPDATE DATABASE MANAGER CONFIGURATION command completed
successfully.
```

Syntax 2: Set the "tcpip" communication protocol for the current Instance.

```
db2set DB2COMM=tcpip
```

Syntax 3: Stop and start the current Instance to get updated values from database manager configuration.

```
db2stop
db2start
```

Updating an Instance

You can update an instance using the following command,:

```
db2iupdt
```

This command is used to update the Instance within the same version release. Before executing this command, you need to stop the Instance database manager using the "db2stop" command. The following syntax "inst_name" indicates the previously released or installed Db2 server Instance name, which you want to update to a newly released or installed Db2 server version.

Syntax 1: To update an instance in normal mode

```
db2iupdt <inst_name>
```

Example:

```
./db2iupdt db2inst2
```

Syntax 2: To update an Instance in debugging mode

```
db2iupdt -D <inst_name>
```

Example:

```
db2iupdt -D db2inst2
```

Upgrading an Instance

You can upgrade an instance from a previous version of a Db2 copy to a newly installed version of a Db2 copy:

```
db2iupgrade
```

On a Linux or UNIX system, this command is located in the DB2DIR/instance directory. In the following syntax, "inst_name" indicates the previous version of the Db2 Instance, and "inst_username" indicates the currently installed version of a Db2 copy for the Instance user:

```
db2iupgrade -d -k -u <inst_username> <inst_name>
```

Example:

```
db2iupgrade -d -k -u db2inst2 db2inst2
```

Command parameters:

-d : Turns debugging mode on

-k : Keeps the pre-upgrade Instance type if it is supported in the
Db2 copy, from which you are running this command

If you are using the super user (su) on Linux for the db2iupgrade command, you must issue the "su" command with the "-" option.

Dropping an Instance

You can drop or delete an instance, which was created by the "db2icrt" command:

```
db2idrop
```

On Linux and UNIX operating systems, this command is located in the DB2_installation_folder/instance directory.

Syntax:

```
db2idrop -u <inst_username> <inst_name>
```

Example:

```
./db2idrop -u db2inst2 db2inst2
```

Using Other Commands with an Instance

The following is the command to find out which Db2 instance we are working on now.

Syntax 1:

```
db2 get instance
```

Output:

```
The current database manager instance is:  db2inst1
```

Syntax 2:

```
db2pd -inst | head -2
```

Example:

```
db2pd -inst | head -2
```

Output:

```
Instance db2inst1 uses 64 bits and DB2 code release SQL10010
```

Syntax 3:

```
db2 select inst_name from sysibmadm.env_inst_info
```

Example:

```
db2 select inst_name from sysibmadm.env_inst_info
```

Output:

```
INST_NAME   --------------------------------------
db2inst1
1 record(s) selected.
```

Syntax 4:

```
db2set db2instdef=<inst_name> -g
```

Example:

```
db2set db2instdef=db2inst2 -g
```

Databases

Databases are the next level of manageable objects in Db2. Every database is contained inside of a single Instance, but there can be multiple databases contained inside an Instance.

The database has no communications interface to the outside world. Instead, the Instance controls communications between each contained database and the outside world. This reduces the redundancy of the communication code when multiple databases are owned by the Instance.

A database contains a large group of objects that together make up both the administration and the storage locations for the database. A partial list of these objects is as follows:

- The database catalogs
- The global deadlock files
- Tablespace information
- Storage group control files
- Temporary tablespaces
- Global configuration file

- History files

- Logging files

- Automated storage containers

Each one of these objects will be discussed at length in the following sections and in Chapter 4 later in this book.

Db2 Catalog Views

The Db2 catalog tables are used to hold information about all the database tables, views, indexes, and other entities contained in the database. Each database contains its own catalog tables, and they are not shared with any other database.

The catalog tables are extremely important and should only be updated by the Db2 system. To that end, you can no longer even read the catalog tables. Instead, the system creates a read-only view of each table. To read a catalog table, you must use the view; you cannot read the catalog tables directly.

The current 11.x release of Db2 contains 140 catalog views plus 9 other views containing statistical information. Many of these views contain very useful information for both administrators and advanced users. Thus, the catalog views are read-only for everyone who has control privileges to that portion of the database. For instance, if a user has no read permissions on a database table, information on that table will not be available to the user in catalog views.

For more detailed information on catalog views, see the IBM documentation at

```
www.ibm.com/support/knowledgecenter/SSEPGG_11.1.0/com.ibm.db2.luw.sql.ref.
doc/doc/r0008443.html
```

This documentation details the complete layout of each view with additional information about all possible values for many columns.

Locking Event Monitor

New in Db2 11 is the locking event monitor. This replaces the deprecated deadlock event monitor. The old monitor had many deficiencies, which caused some deadlocks to not be detected. The new logging event monitor is much better at detecting deadlocks as they occur instead of waiting for some kind of deadlock timeout. It provides a more robust system to users and administrators.

Deadlock information can be written to two different database tables, but it is always in binary format. Choosing between these two tables can be tricky, so careful thought should be given to your choice. By using SQL to query the table, the system will interpret the binary data and translate to a supported language such as English.

Enabling the locking event monitor is automatic when you execute the CREATE statement for it. The following statement will enable the locking event monitor:

```
create event monitor for locking
```

When a deadlock is detected, the following information is collected in the event log:

- The lock that resulted in the event

- The application holding the lock that resulted in the lock event

- The applications that were waiting for or requesting the lock that resulted in the lock event

- What the applications were doing during the lock event

Tablespace Information

Tablespaces are used to contain database tables. When a database is created, three tablespaces are created automatically. The first tablespace, SYSCATSPACE, contains the database catalog and views. The second tablespace, USERSPACE1, is the default space used to hold the database tables. The third, TEMPSPACE1, is used to hold temporary tables for query results. All these tablespaces are created by default in the location specified when the Db2 system was installed.

There is a lot of information on tablespaces, and this book has an entire chapter devoted to that topic. See Chapter 4 for more information.

The basic command for obtaining tablespace information is as follows:

```
mon_get_tablespace (tblsp_name, member)
```

If the tblsp_name is NULL or an empty string, then all tablespaces will be returned.

The member specifies the member number of the tablespace. If it is –1, the current member information is returned. If it is –2, then all member information is returned. If NULL is specified, it is the same as specifying –1.

Storage Group Control Files

Storage groups are an intermediate level between the database and its tablespaces. You use storage groups to group together tablespaces. This allows a whole set of tablespaces to reside in the same location. A database can have many storage groups spread across any number of disk devices.

Unless you specify otherwise, a default storage group is created when you create a database. All of the tablespaces will reside in that storage group. See Chapter 4 for more information.

Global Configuration File

The global configuration file is created by an administrator. It is used to set backup procedures for the Db2 system. See the IBM documentation for more information.

History Files

History files are instance specific and are stored in the same place as the instance information. They contain some global information on the instance like the last start and stop times and other sometimes useful data. The number of these files can change from release to release, so refer to your release-specific documentation for more information.

Logging Files

The logging files are specific to a database and store information logged by the Db2 system. The number and types of the files will be specific to your database configuration.

Automated Storage Containers

These are discussed at length in Chapter 4. A default storage container is created when a database is created.

Creating a Database

When a database is created, it is automatically attached to the current instance, that is, the instance you are currently logged into. If this is the very first database ever created, a new default instance will be created for you. The default owner of the database is always the administrator who creates the database. All database system tables are placed in the default storage group known as "IBMSTOGROUP."

There are two types of database that can be created, a restrictive and a nonrestrictive database. The difference between the two databases is the restrictive database is not granted the "PUBLIC" privilege. This means that only database administrators have access to a restrictive database.

The default privileges on all database tables are CREATETAB, BINDADD, CONNECT, IMPLICIT_SCHEMA, and SELECT. Nonrestrictive databases also have the PUBLIC privilege. These privileges apply to all tables in the database.

To create a nonrestrictive database, use the following syntax:

```
db2 create database [dbname]
```

The dbname is the name of the database to be created. It must be unique for all databases managed by Db2. The following is an example:

```
$ db2 create database mydb
DB20000I The CREATE DATABASE command completed successfully.
```

To create a restrictive database, use the following syntax:

```
db2 create database [dbname] restrictive
```

The dbname is the name of the database to be created. It must be unique for all databases managed by Db2. The following is an example:

```
$ db2 create database myrestrict db restrictive
DB20000I The CREATE DATABASE command completed successfully.
```

Databases do not have to be created in the default location, that is, the default tablespace can be located anywhere in the server's file system. To place a database in the location of your choice, use the following syntax:

```
db2 create database [dbname] [restrictive] on 'dblocation' dbpath on 'path_
location'
```

This will create the database in the folder /path_location/dblocation. Note that the final file path is reversed from the way it is shown in the statement syntax.

Listing Databases

To see the list of databases contained in the current instance, use the following command:

```
$ db2 list database directory
```

The following is an example partial listing of the output of this command:

```
System Database Directory
Number of entries in the directory      = 6
Database 1 entry:
  Database alias                        = FOUR
  Database name                         = FOUR
  Local database directory              = /home/db2inst4/Desktop/dbpath
  Database release level                = f.00
  Comment                               =
  Directory entry type                  = Indirect
  Catalog database partition number     = 0
  Alternate server hostname             =
  Alternate server port number          =
Database 2 entry:
  Database alias                        = SIX
  Local database directory              = /home/db2inst4
  Database release level                = f.00
  Comment                               =
  Directory entry type                  = Indirect
  Catalog database partition number     = 0
  Alternate server hostname             =
  Alternate server port number          =
```

You should note here the different paths to each database. It demonstrates how you can distribute databases throughout the file system of the server.

Activating a Database

To activate a database, use the following syntax:

```
db2 activate db [dbname]
```

The dbname is the name of the database to be activated.

You should note that this is different from the db2start command. That command activates all databases in an instance, whereas this command only activates a single database. No matter which command is used, all the necessary processes and threads are activated within the instance.

Deactivating a Database

To deactivate a single database in the instance, use the following syntax:

```
db2 deactivate dn [dbname]
```

This will stop a single database named dbname. If this is the only active database, then all the processes and threads for the instance will also be stopped.

Connecting to a Database

To connect to a database, use the following syntax:

```
db2 connect to [dbname]
```

This will connect you to the database named dbname. You can now issue SQL commands to the database.

Dropping a Database

To drop a database, use the following syntax:

```
Db2 drop database [dbname]
```

The dbname is the name of the database. Note that even if this is the only database contained within the instance, the instance will not be dropped.

Tables

Tables are the linchpin of all relational databases. They hold the data that we want to save and organize, no matter what kind of data it might be. Tables are what makes a relational database different from other kinds of databases.

When first encountered, you may think of them as a kind of spreadsheet, and that is a logical analogy. But they have some fundamental differences that set them apart. First, they have a limited number of columns. Second, each column is limited to a single data type. Third, one or more of the columns have a relationship to columns in other table(s), in most cases. The third case is what defines the relational database. Relationships between columns are the key to unlocking both visible and hidden relationships between tables. This is key to discovering interesting things about the data that may have been previously unknown or not obvious.

Tables are made up of columns and rows. While the columns in each row will contain data of the same data type, the values in each column of a row will be mostly different. The number of rows in a table is not necessarily determined by any factor except what is needed by the kind of data being stored and the application(s) using the data.

The number of tables in a database is only determined by the needs of the data itself. The database administrator has the responsibility to determine the organization and number of tables. There are a number of factors that go into this analysis, and all have an impact on the design of a database. Just some of these factors are listed in the following:

1. Usability: The database must be as easy to use as possible. Many times there will be users of the data that have limited training on how to create efficient queries, and these must be taken into account.

2. Reporting: There will always be the need to create reports form the data contained in the database. The structure of the data should make this as easy and efficient as possible.

3. Security: The relational database has some really great mechanisms to secure the data it stores. This needs to be designed such that only the data needed by a user is actually available to them.

4. Support and development: The database needs to be designed so that it is easy to maintain with minimal staff. This could mean that during development, some extra time and human resources are needed to accomplish this goal.

5. Functionality: The database is there to solve problems and reveal things previously unknown to the user group. The design of the database needs to accommodate this need.

6. Integration: The database must not only fit into the organization's infrastructure, but it must accommodate possible new innovation in the infrastructure itself. It must also anticipate new databases being integrated into the infrastructure.

7. Cost: Is the database cost effective? Will it continue to be cost effective? These questions must be answered, sometimes by changing the design of the database. In other cases, different changes may be needed.

8. Scalability: Is the database scalable? What happens when the amount of data doubles or quadruples? What happens when the organization changes (either the data or the organization)? All these questions should be answered with considerations toward cost, efficiency, and performance.

9. Hosting: What kind of hardware will be hosting the database? Can it be spread across multiple systems? All of this will have a direct impact on hardware and support costs.

10. Updates: This is often ignored and left to the support personnel to figure out. This is a grievous mistake. Relational database are all different concerning system updates. Some systems require to be completely halted to apply updates, some require a reboot to apply updates, and others can continue to run even as updates are being applied. In any case, there are always "gotchas" for each update process.

The design of a database from a task perspective is mostly about the design of the tables and their layout. This process will be discussed at length in Chapter 4.

Table Types

There are three major table types in Db2. These are

- Base tables: These tables are the ones that all users will know and use. They hold persistent data.

- Temporary tables: Some types of queries will require the creation of temporary tables. These tables never appear in the system in the system catalog and can never have XML columns. As the name implies, these tables are temporary in nature and are destroyed when the transaction closes.

- Materialized query tables: These tables are used for performance improvements in queries. They are defined by the query, which also determines what is stored in them. These tables are also destroyed by the system when the transaction closes.

The base table type is the one used by everyone. The other two table types are mostly used by more highly trained individuals for specialized reporting needs. Both of these tables are like the base tables in that they both use the standard data types, which we will look at next.

Built-in Data Types

There are a number of very useful built-in data types in Db2. In addition to these, you can define your own data types, but we will not cover those in this book.

The Db2 built-in data types and their definitions are listed in the following:

- TIME: Represents the time of day in hours, minutes, and seconds. All the parts are numeric.

- TIMESTAMP: Represents a specific date and time through seven values in the form of year, month, day, hours, minutes, seconds, and microseconds. All the parts are numeric.

- DATE: Represents the date in three parts in the form of year, month, and day. All the parts are numeric.

- CHAR(fixed length): Represents a fixed-length character string. Strings shorter than the fixed length will have blanks appended to them when assigned to this data type. The length of the defined string must be 0 < fixed length < 256.

- VARCHAR(max length): Represents a variable-length string. The defined length must be less than 32763.

- LONG VARCHAR: Represents a variable-length string up to 500k in length.

- CLOB: Represents large character blocks up to 500k in length.

- GRAPHIC(length): This is a binary type of graphic data up to 500k in length.

- VARGRAPHIC(max length): This is a binary type of graphic data up to a max of 500k in length.

- DBCLOB: Represents a double-byte binary string of up to 500k in length.

- BLOB(max length): Represents a binary blob string of up to 500k in length.

- BOOLEAN: Represents a Boolean value of either 0 or 1.

- SMALLINT: Represents a small signed integer (a signed 16-bit value).

- INTEGER: Represents a signed integer (a signed 32-bit value).

- BIGINT: Represents a large signed integer (a signed 64-bit value).

- DECIMAL(p,s) or DEC(p,s): A signed decimal number specified by p and s. p is the precision, or the number of decimal digits, up to 31 digits. s is the scale of the digits, or the number of digits to the right of the decimal point, in the range of $1-10^{**}31$ to $10^{**}31-1$.

- NUMERIC(p,s): Same as DECIMAL(p,s).

- REAL: Represents a single-precision floating-point number.

- DOUBLE: Represents a double-precision floating-point number.

- XML: Represents a well-formed XML document. There is not an effective size limit to the document except when it is transmitted to another Db2 server. Here the size limit is 2 GB.

Creating a Table

The SQL statement for creating a table is not used by many standard users, but it is used by database administrators. Users can create materialized query tables (MQTs), but only administrators can create regular tables. The SQL statement for both kinds of tables is essentially the same with only minor differences.

To begin our discussion of tables, we should take a look at the syntax for the CREATE TABLE SQL statement in Listing 3-1.

Listing 3-1. The CREATE TABLE SQL Statement Syntax

```
CREATE TABLE [Tablename]
( [Column | Unique Constraint | Referential Constraint | Check Constraint],
... )
<LIKE [Source] <CopyOptions>>
<IN [TS_Name]>
<INDEX IN [TS_Name}>
<LONG IN [TS_Name]>
<ORGANIZE BY [ROW | COLUMN]>
<PARTITION BY [PartitionClause]>
<COMPRESS [YES | NO]>
```

The hard part of this statement is the list of columns/constraints. Essentially this is the list of columns the table contains. The list is read from top to bottom, and this turns into a left-to-right list in a SELECT * statement. Each column will always have one of the associated built-in data types described in the previous section or one of the defined data types usually created by the database admin. We will discuss how columns are defined later in this section.

Following the list of columns are all the table options. We will not discuss all of these options except the ones that have an associated tablespace name (TS_Name). This is unique in a few relational database systems including Db2. Tablespaces are always defined on a particular disk drive or a set of drives. This allows a busy table to be placed on one or more disk drives that is at least somewhat dedicated to the tables in the tablespace. The IN, INDEX IN, and LONG IN clauses specify the tablespace in which the table and/or index will be placed. The table and the index do not have to be in the same tablespace.

The following are a few examples of a CREATE TABLE statement:

```
create table employee (
     id integer,
     name varchar(50),
     jobrole varchar(30),
     joindate date,
     salary decimal(10, 2))
in ts1
```

This is a very standard CREATE TABLE statement for the employee defining five columns. There are no indexes or constraints defined for this table. It is placed in a defined tablespace named ts1.

```
create table parts (
     id integer primary key not null,
     name varchar(50) not null,
     price (decimal 6, 2),
     description char(50) not null)
```

The parts table defined here has several columns defined with the NOT NULL keywords. This specifies that the column will not allow a NULL value to be stored in it. The id column is defined as the PRIMARY KEY of the table, and thus an index of that column's values will be created. You should note that the index for this column is not **unique** as it does not specify the UNIQUE keyword. Last, since no tablespace has been specified, the tables and indexes will be placed in the default tablespace.

There are many options for the CREATE TABLE statement, many more than we can document here. Just assume the options for the Db2 statement are different from other relational database systems you may be familiar with and do not assume you know the syntax since you know system X's syntax.

The full syntax of the CREATE TABLE statement is available online on the IBM website. Just search for "db2 create table syntax" in your favorite web search engine.

Alter a Table

The ALTER TABLE and ALTER COLUMN statements are able to make changes to a table in a somewhat limited manner. For instance, the ALTER COLUMN statement may only change the ability of a column to store/not store NULLS under certain circumstances.

What these statements can do is add/remove columns, drop tables/indexes, and change referential integrity constraints and a few other items.

All of these limitations apply to normal tables as well as MQTs. However, the ALTER statements are not limited to administrators for MQTs. Users with permissions can ALTER an MQT.

It is suggested that you look up the syntax of the ALTER statements before attempting to use them. These statements are not used very often, so do not assume you remember the details of the syntax.

Other Table SQL Statements

There are some other SQL statements that can supply you with information about a table. With these statements, you have to have at least "read" permissions in order for the system to provide you information about a table, tablespace, index, or any other entity you wish to query.

To see a list of table details related to schemas and tablespaces, use the following:

```
select tabname, tabschema, tbspace from syscat.tables
```

This will list all the database table names, tables schemas (if any), and tablespace names that hold the tables.

To see the list of columns in a table, use the following:

```
describe table parts
```

This will show all the columns in the parts table along with the data types and attributes of each column.

Dropping a Table

The SQL statement to delete a table no longer in use is the DROP statement. You should note that any data contained by the table will be lost after you DROP the table. By default, the triggers and relations for a table are NOT dropped.

The following statement will drop the `parts` table:

```
drop table parts
```

To drop the hierarchy of triggers and relations and the table at the same time, use the following:

```
drop table heirarchy parts
```

This SQL statement (both versions) is limited to the owner of the table, usually a database administrator.

Summary

This chapter has presented a variety of Db2 management commands that are used frequently by a Db2 administrator. These commands have a number of syntax variations, which can be used to add, alter, or remove Db2 objects from the database including the database itself, tables, indexes, and other entities.

CHAPTER 4

Database Physical Design

The physical design of a relational database is a two-phase project. The first phase involves the design of the tables and their relationships. The second phase lays out the table design onto the physical drives provided by the system. Both of these phases are necessary for proper optimization of the database information. But there are inevitable conflicts between the two phases that will need to be resolved during performance testing.

This chapter will cover each of these phases and highlight where possible conflicts can reduce performance of the database. Do not be put off by the concepts covered in this chapter. These topics will only be covered in the depth necessary for a good understanding of where things can go wrong. Programmers may think that this chapter does not apply to them, but they would be wrong in that assumption. Programmers need to understand the choices made by the database designers so that they can properly compose their SQL statements to make the best use of the design.

Phase 1 of the physical design of a relational database involves gathering the data and a process known as normalization of the data. Normalization is the process of organizing table data in such a way as to reduce the dependencies on other data either within the same table or other tables. The normalization process has three steps. Each step puts a table into first normal form, second normal form, or third normal form. All of these steps involve establishing creating tables to contain just the data needed to make it useful to the users. The depth to which that is taken determines the level of the normalization.

Phase 2 of the physical design places the tables created in Phase 1 and their corresponding tablespaces onto a physical drive. The drive might be one of the new SSD memory devices or a spinning disk or RAID system. Less used data may even be placed on even slower media or a remote system. The type of media used for storage is strictly determined by the performance requirements of the data being stored.

© W. David Ashley 2021
W. D. Ashley, *Foundation Db2 and Python*, https://doi.org/10.1007/978-1-4842-6942-8_4

The basic problem for the database designer(s) is to balance the needs of the users with the system and media available for the database. This really means that both phases should be done together. Performing each phase individually risks one of the phases impacting the other phase in ways that may cause the previous phase to be partially redone.

Phase 1: Data Gathering and Normalization

This phase gathers the data that will make up the database and then normalizes it. This phase is also known as the logical model of the data.

One thing that needs to be made clear for this phase is that the users of the data need to be heavily involved in gathering and organizing the data for the database. If nothing else, this will help you discover the kind of queries that will be made on the data. The queries will help you to organize the data in such a way that both improves query performance and creates a design that is both logical and helpful to the users.

Data Gathering

This task may involve a number of groups, especially if the data is coming from an existing source. The following is a list of potential groups that may need to be involved in gathering the data:

- The end users of the database to be designed

  This group of people will be using the data contained by your database. They may also have insights from any existing source data for the new database. They may/may not design queries, but they have expectations for the information they can gain from the data.

- Owners of the source data for the database

  This group are the owners of any source data to be used for the new database. If any changes/additions to this data are necessary, you will need to notify and give ownership of these requested changes to this group.

- The group that maintains the physical hardware for the database

This group will be the maintainers of the physical hardware housing the database. As the size of the new database becomes known, this group will be responsible for maintaining that hardware. Also, if hardware needs to be purchased, this group will most likely be involved in the purchasing and installation of the hardware.

- The group responsible for data backup

This group maintains any backups and restore images for the new database. Hardware may need to be purchased and installed for this task, so this group will need to be in the loop for that task.

- IT management for the database

Management will need to be involved to approve any new hardware purchase and/or new personnel for database maintenance.

As you can see, there are any number of people involved in designing a database. In your organization, there may even be other groups that need to be brought in at different points in the process.

Data gathering involves an array of potential sources depending on the type of data. The sources could involve other databases, data on tapes, online sources, automated inputs, manual data entry inputs, and even sources from other companies or governmental agencies. How all of your sources deliver the data can have an impact on the timeliness of the data and could have an impact on the queries made on the database.

Once you have an idea of the data coming in, it will be time to organize it. You and the final users will need to define the potential entities easily recognized in the data. In addition, you may be able to reorganize the data to form new entities that better reflect the organization of the data. Of course, when it comes time to create the table organization, you may need additional tables and/or indexes that the users will not use directly to maintain the data/table relationships.

Any table organization you create at this time should be considered temporary. This should be made very clear to your users. There is still a long way to go before the design is stable, and everyone should be aware of this.

Data Normalization

Normalization involves removing redundancies from your tables and removing entities from your tables that are not actually an attribute of the table entity. This is very much like organizing a table in the same way you would design an OOP class definition. Things that are not attributes of the main table entity should be removed from the table. Usually one or more new tables will need to be created to hold this removed data.

Normalization involves three forms, or steps:

- First normal form: The information is stored in a table with each column containing atomic values. There are no repeating groups of columns.

- Second normal form: The tables are in first normal form, and all the columns depend on the primary key.

- Third normal form: The table is stored in second normal form, and all of its columns are not transitively dependent on the primary key.

First Normal Form

First normal form involves checking if any column is a combination of any two or more of the other columns or if there are repeated columns with the same or similar information.

For instance, a column that contains two other columns added together falls into this category. It turns out that it is very easy for the database to perform this calculation for a query, so a summary column is considered redundant. The same would apply to string data columns concatenated together to form a third column. Always let the database perform this data transformation for you. One thing this will prevent is potential data corruption when one of the columns involved in the transformation is updated with a new value.

Let's take a look at a table that contains summary data:

```
CREATE TABLE employee (
    VARCHAR(50) name NOT NULL,
    . . .
    DECIMAL(10,2) salary,
    DECIMAL(10,2) bonus,
```

```
DECIMAL(10,2) total_salary,
. . .
);
```

When the employee is created, the salary and bonus are known, and the input for the total_salary is calculated. This is not first normal form because we have a field contained in the table that is calculated from two other fields in the table. This is very prone to errors later on when either the salary or the bonus is updated and the total_salary is forgotten. This will obviously cause a referential integrity problem. In this case, the total_salary field should be removed, and if that value is needed later on, have the database add the salary and bonus fields together during the query. This will have very little impact on the query and preserves referential integrity.

Our second example involves keeping repeated information in a table that is not directly related to the main table entity. The following is an example of such a table:

```
CREATE TABLE customer (
    . .
    VARCHAR(50) name NOT NULL,
    . . .
    INT ordernum1,
    INT ordernum2,
    INT ordernum3,
    . . .
)
```

The idea here is that the last three orders for a customer are kept with the customer data for convenience. This is bad because the order of the three order numbers must be kept intact. This turns out to be really hard to do. The database can easily pull the most recent orders from the order table, so you should let it do its job and remove these fields from the customer table.

Second Normal Form

Second normal form removes any column that does not depend on the table's primary key. This will prevent any partial dependencies between table fields. For instance, you would not store a customer order in the table that stores the customer information. A separate order table should be created to hold this information. After all, a customer may have multiple active orders at any time.

The following is an example of a violation of second normal form:

```
CREATE TABLE part (
    VARCHAR(50) partnum PRIMARY KEY NOT NULL,
    VARCHAR(50) warehouse PRIMARY KEY NOT NULL,
    INT quantity NOT NULL,
    VARCHAR(50) warehouse_addr NOT NULL
    )
```

In this example, the warehouse_addr is not an attribute of part. It is an attribute of the warehouse table, so it does not belong in the part table.

Third Normal Form

Third normal form is a little harder to recognize. A good example of this would be a hospital database where patient data is stored. If the patient table contains the doctor's phone number, then that data does not depend on the patient. That data belongs to the doctor table. That column should be replaced by a key reference to the doctor, not an attribute of the doctor entity. This is known as removing a transitive dependency.

The following example shows how a violation of third normal form can cause referential integrity problems:

```
CREATE TABLE employee (
    INT emp_num PRIMARY KEY NOT NULL,
    VARCHAR(20) first_name NOT NULL,
    VARCHAR(20) last_name NOT NULL,
    CHAR(10) work_dept NOT NULL,
    VARCHAR(20) dept_name NOT NULL
    )
```

If the dept_name needs to be changed (but not the work_dept), then if you miss a single employee in that department, you now have a referential integrity problem. The dept_name belongs to the department table, not the employee table, so that column should be removed.

One last thing to point out is that third normal form, when implemented, can cause performance problems. Many database designers have taken their designs to third normal form only to find that they have to fall back so that the data is directly in a table that is not in third normal form to have proper performance for the users.

Fourth Normal Form

There is a fourth normal form, but we will not discuss this as it requires new tables
to be created to resolve the problem. This can sometimes lead to both confusion and
frustration on the users creating queries. This hassle may or may not be worth it for your
database. The exception might be for really large databases where space is at a premium
because fourth normal form can reduce the space needed by the database.

Business Rules

Once you have the major tables designed, it is time to consider the business rules that
will be needed to automatically keep tables in sync. This activity will ease the process of
adding and updating your tables. Several tables may have direct relationships that need
to be maintained. If a new row is added to a table, there may have to be dependencies
that also need to be maintained. Business rules can ease this task by making automatic
updates/additions/deletions when a dependent table is updated.

Db2 has many facilities to help in these cases. There are so many of them that we
have devoted a whole chapter to cover them. Refer to Chapter 6.

Phase 2: Physical Design of the Database

Once you have the tables, indexes, and business rules designed, you need to lay out the
tables on a set of disk drives. There are a number of ways to do this depending on the
hardware you have to work with and the size of your database.

A small database, one up to a few gigabytes, can easily be placed on a single disk
drive without a major performance penalty. However, the task gets harder the larger
the database becomes. If you start with a small database and it begins to grow, then
performance becomes a major concern. So not only should you consider the size of the
database today, you also need to be aware about its potential growth rate and design an
appropriate solution.

In the old days when disk drives were rather small and performance restricted,
even a small database needed to be designed around the performance of the disk
drives. A single table might need to span several drives so that they could work together
asynchronously on a query. Today, drives are enormous in size, some even 8 and 10 TB

in size, and getting larger all the time. Beware of these drives. Trying to use all the space available on these drives can cause huge performance impacts just because of the seek time on the disk.

A lot of the problems with big disk drives can be resolved to some extent by creating a RAID array. RAIDs 5 and 6 are fairly good alternatives where the data in a table can be spread across all the drives in the array. Thus, if eight drives make up the array, then all eight might be tasked to work on retrieving data from a table. But there are potential problems with this solution. In the early days, there were big performance problems when writing data to an array. These penalties have been partly eliminated over the years, but in some respects they still exist.

RAID 6 was an attempt to eliminate the write performance penalties of RAID 5. To a large extent, the implementation succeeded without adding new penalties or increasing penalties to existing features. The main penalty to RAID 6 is the larger overhead needed to accommodate storage space for cache and temporary storage. This, as it turns out, can be completely ignored on larger sets of today's disks. With their larger sizes, today's disks can easily accommodate the necessary overhead.

The solution that mainframes use is to use a single or a set of drives to store a large single table. But this is not a good solution for small- and midsize systems because with drives of today, there will be a lot of wasted space on the drive(s).

One relatively new kind of drive that is now available can resolve some of these problems. These are the SSDs and other memory-based drives. These drives have outstanding performance for both reading and writing. However, they are still relatively small in size, and the cost can be prohibitive to purchase a large number of them. But in the future, these may become the drive of choice for many databases because the performance is so good.

Backups

This is the time to start thinking about backups of your database. Don't put this task off until later as that will cause you headaches and problems later on. If you are doing backups to disk, you will require additional disk space to accommodate them. For tape, you may need a dedicated tape drive for the database. The size of your database may determine your backup options. All this needs to be considered up front during the design process, not later.

Db2 has a dedicated backup command run from the db2 prompt. You should use this command if at all possible as it has encryption and compression options, as well as being able to perform incremental backups. It has multiple options for performing all different kinds of backups at the database, page, and tablespace levels. It can perform backups to any device as long as it is mounted to the file system. The one exception to this is performing a backup to another Db2 remote database. This can be done over a number of connections to the local system.

Do not try to finalize your backup solution during the planning process. The idea is to size your option and try to select an option that can be finalized later.

Summary

This chapter has given a high-level overview of the tasks necessary to collect the data necessary and then perform a first-level logical and physical design of your database. We covered all the major topics for accomplishing this goal with the appropriate people making contributions to that effort.

It should be remembered this has only been a short review. You should consult additional material should you actually be tasked with this job. What we have presented here is only a guide to the high-level tasks.

CHAPTER 5

Db2 Utilities

In this chapter, we will introduce the Db2 utilities. The utilities help to manage the databases, tablespaces, tables, and indexes owned by the Db2 system. These utilities include backup, import, export, load, reorg, runstats, rebind, move, and a few other commands. We will cover many of these commands in this chapter.

Normally you would log into the instance of Db2 that you want to run the utility command under and then run the command from that point. If you are logged in as the owner of the Db2 instance, you can also run commands from the operating system command prompt as follows:

```
[db2inst1@centos dashley]$ db2 db2start
```

This command will start the first instance of Db2 from the Linux command line. The Windows command prompt will be similar to this. Any utility command can be run in this way, which means you can code your commands in a script and run it from the instance owner's command line. Doing it this way will ensure that you have not forgotten a Db2 utility command-line option you may consistently need.

The Db2 utilities are NOT simple commands. In some cases, they seem to have dozens of options and can be very intimidating at first glance. Instead of trying to explain every option, we will discuss only the options you are likely to use in most cases. This will reduce the complexity of the command for you while covering the most used options. Should you need other option(s), you should consult the Db2 online documentation for the option(s) you require.

For much more information, refer to the proper online PDF manual at the following URL:

```
www.ibm.com/support/pages/node/627743
```

© W. David Ashley 2021
W. D. Ashley, *Foundation Db2 and Python*, https://doi.org/10.1007/978-1-4842-6942-8_5

Backup Command

The `backup` command is not usually considered when discussing the Db2 utilities. We consider this such an important topic that it deserves front and center attention when discussing the complete set of Db2 utilities. Without a clear and complete plan for backing up your database and the recovery of the data, you are setting yourself up for disaster. You need to have a plan that has been fully tested to assure that your data is completely safe. Always remember that backups are useless if you have not verified that the data can also be restored.

For much more information concerning a `backup,` please refer to the IBM online Db2 manual at the following URL:

www.ibm.com/support/knowledgecenter/SSEPGG_11.5.0/com.ibm.db2.luw.welcome.doc/doc/welcome.html

The companion to the `backup` command is the `restore` command, which is covered later in this chapter.

What Is a Backup?

A typical backup strategy involves two kinds of backup – full and partial. Whatever backup you choose, be aware that the resulting data files will be in binary form and are unsuitable for extracting data for reports or any other human-readable use. Both full and partial backups are an exact copy of the data as it exists within the database and thus consume the exact amount of file space as the data held in the database.

Because of the method of extraction of the data from the database, the utility does not use or store SQL to perform the extraction of the data. From the perspective of the user/administrator, this means that a backup, full or partial, should not be considered a "database dump" because it contains no data that can be used to recreate the table(s) or index(es). The primary use of a backup is as a source for the `restore` command in case of a disaster recovery or a disk failure or for moving the data to a new database. The database administrator should be in charge of providing a database backup strategy that meets the needs of the data, application, and the besiness requirements.

The `restore` command is the bookend to the `backup` command. A `backup`/`restore` is nearly always the fastest way to get a whole database from one place to another, especially without much preplanning.

Backup Verification

For production databases, it is critical that a backup be verified to ensure that it is valid. The tool for this is called db2ckbkp. This tool verifies the backup image to ensure the validity of the image. The syntax for this looks like

```
db2 db2ckbkp image_file_name
```

An example of its output looks like this:

```
[db2inst1@centos dashley]$ db2ckbkp SAMPLE.0.DB2.
DBPART000.20190318184324.001

[1] Buffers processed:   #######

Image Verification Complete - successful.
```

Verification may run as long as the original backup image took. As a database backup image grows, there are more pound signs produced in the preceding example. When you are really depending on a particular database backup image is when you want to run this command. If the data is critical enough, then you should consider storing a copy of every verified backup on a different storage device than the database.

Advanced Backup Options

There are many more options you can use on the backup command. You should refer to the IBM Knowledge Center online reference mentioned earlier in this section.

Backup Syntax

This section is about the syntax of the backup command. Although the complete syntax for the command will be shown, we will not cover every option in detail. Instead, we will show a number of examples that should cover the most likely uses of the command.

The **BACKUP DATABASE** command creates a backup copy of a database or a tablespace. A backup of your database and related stored data should be created to prevent data loss if a database outage occurs.

When performing a partitioned backup is specified, the command can be called only on the catalog database partition. If the option specifies that all database partition servers are to be backed up, all of the database partition servers that are listed in the db2nodes.cfg file will be backed up. Otherwise, only the database partition servers that are specified on the command will be affected.

Command Syntax

```
BACKUP [DATABASE | DB] [DatabaseAlias]
  [USER [Username] [Using [password]]]
  [TABLESPACE (TbspNames]) | NO TABLESPACE]
  [ONLINE]
  [INCREMENTAL [DELTA]]
  [TO [Location] | USE TSM [OPTIONS [TSMOptions]]]
  [WITH [NumBuffers] BUFFERS]
  [BUFFER [BufferSize]]
  [PARALLELISM [parallelNum]]
  [COMPRESS]
  [UTIL_IMPACT_PRIORITY [Priority]]
  [INCLUDE LOGS | EXCLUDE LOGS]
  [WITHOUT PROMPTING]
```

The backup command is extremely flexible. It is possible to back up a complete database, one or more tablespaces, and an incremental copy of a database or tablespaces. The backup file containing the backup data can be saved to TSM or to a file system. You can also choose to back up the logs with the data.

How It Works

The backup command does NOT utilize SQL when performing the backup. It operates at the file system level. This means that it is the fastest method of backing up your database or tablespaces. This also means that it has the most impact on the database when run with the database up and running. The potential for collisions during a backup with an active database is very probable; thus, the performances will not be optimal. But if the database has light usages, the impact will be much smaller.

Usage Notes

- Backups should be stored on media not directly connected to the server where the Db2 database resides. This will protect your data should a hardware or server fault occur.

- Snapshot backups should be complemented with regular disk backups in case of failure in the file/storage system.

- Recent versions of the Db2 backup command have the INCLUDE LOGS option set as the default. Older versions of the backup utility have the EXCLUDE LOGS option as the default.

- Always test not only the backups you make but also the restore of those backups. The backup files are of no use if they cannot be restored.

Export Command

The EXPORT command exports data from a database to one of several external file formats, all in an ASCII format. The user specifies the data to be exported by supplying an SQL SELECT statement or by providing hierarchical information for typed tables.

For more information concerning an export, please refer to the IBM online Db2 manual at the following URL:

www.ibm.com/support/knowledgecenter/SSEPGG_11.5.0/com.ibm.db2.luw.welcome.doc/doc/welcome.html

The export command is not as fast as the backup command because it uses SQL to select the data to be exported. It should be used when you want a selective partial backup of only some of the database data. It should also be noted that the data from export cannot be used to restore the database to a previous state as no information about a database state is exported in the data.

The import command is the companion to the export command. It is covered later in this chapter.

Command syntax

```
DB2 EXPORT TO [Filename] OF [DEL | WSK | IXF]
    [LOBS TO [LOBPath]]
    [LOBFILE [LOBFileName]]
    [XML TO [XMLPath]]
    [XMLFILE [XMLFileName]]
    [MODIFIED BY [Modifiers]]
    [METHOD N ([ColumnNames])]
    [MESSAGES [MSGFileName]]
    [SELECTStatement]
```

The export command removes data from the database and stores it in one of three file formats: DEL, WSJ, or IXF. This IXF format is used almost exclusively for moving data between databases. The export command is most used to remove data from the database that has a fixed time period of usefulness such as tax data, some employee data, etc.

There are a number of options that support LOBs, XML, and messages. All of these can be used to ensure that the data has been exported in the manner you need it.

You should ensure that the SQL statement used in the export command is correct before you perform a final export of the data.

Usage Notes

- All table operations and the release of all locks must be complete before you start an export operation. The best method of accomplishing this is by executing a COMMIT after you close all cursors opened with the WITH HOLD option or by issuing a ROLLBACK.

- The PC/IXF format must be used to move data between databases. If character data that contains row separators is exported to a delimited ASCII DEL, the data could be modified with a file transfer such that row separators could be added during the transfer.

Import Command

The import command inserts data from an external file that has a supported file format into a table, hierarchy, view, or nickname. Load is a faster alternative, but the load utility does not support loading data at the hierarchy level.

For more information concerning an import, please refer to the IBM online Db2 manual at the following URL:

www.ibm.com/support/knowledgecenter/SSEPGG_11.5.0/com.ibm.db2.luw.welcome.
doc/doc/welcome.html

The import command uses SQL commands to perform all operations. Thus, it is slower than the load command, but it allows all data checks the database has to enforce.

The companion to the import command is the export command. The export command is covered in this chapter just above this section. The import command can directly use the output of the export command.

Command Syntax

```
IMPORT FROM [Filename] OF [DEL | ASC | WSF | IXF]
  [LOBS FROM [LOBPath]]
  [XML FROM [XMLPath]]
  [MODIFIED BY {Modifiers}]
  [Method]
  [XML PARSE [STRIP | PRESERVE] WHITESPACE]
  [XMLVALIDATION USING [XDS | SCHEMA [SchemaID]]]
  [ALLOW NO ACCESS | ALLOW WRITE ACCESS]
  [COMMITCOUNT [CommitCount] | COMMITCOUNT AUTOMATIC]
  [RESTARTCOUNT | SKIPCOUNT | COMMITCOUNT AUTOMATIC]
  [WARNINGCOUNT [WarningCount]]
  [NOTIMEOUT]
  [MESSAGES [MsgFileName]]
  [CREATE | INSERT | INSERT_UPDATE | REPLACE | REPLACE_CREATE]
    INTO [TableName] <([ColumnName])>]
    [IN [TSName] [INDEX IN [TSName]] [LONG IN [TSName]]]
```

The `import` command can load a database from several different file formats as well as `import` LOBs and XML. You should note that the SQL statement that it supports is very flexible but has a specific format. There are several mechanisms that can control how the data is imported and when to stop the utility due to error conditions.

Load Command

The `load` command efficiently loads large amounts of data into a Db2 table. This command does not use SQL, so no checking of the data is performed. It is also much faster than the `import` command. It is typically used to insert new data into the database.

Since the `load` command loads data at the database page level, it bypasses the firing of triggers and logging. It also delays any constraint checking and index building until after all the data has been loaded into its respective table(s).

The primary use of the `load` command is to insert new data into the database. It can read data from files, devices, or pipes. The command can be set up to run as an hourly, daily, or even continuous feed to the database. Since the utility does not use SQL, care should be taken to eliminate any conflicts with the data or the existing database before inserting it in the database.

While the load command does not use SQL to actually load data into the database, it does use SQL syntax to specify which table/column is to be loaded.

Command Syntax

```
LOAD <CLIENT> FROM [Filename OF [DEL | ASC | IXF] | PipeName | Device |
      CursorName OF CURSOR]
   <LOBS FROM [LOBPath]>
   <MODIFIED BY [Modifiers]>
   <Method>
   <SAVECOUNT [SaveCount]>
   <ROWCOUNT [RowCount]>
   <WARNINGCOUNT [WarningCount]>
   <MESSAGES [MsgFileName]>
   <TEMPFILESPATH [TempFilesPath]>
   <INSERT | REPLACE | RESTART | TERMINATE]
```

```
INTO [TableName] <([ColumnNames])>
<FOR EXCEPTION [ExTableName]>
<STATISTICS [NO | USE PROFILE]>
<NORECOVERABLE | COPY YES TO {CopyLocation | TSM]>
<WITHOUT PROMPTING>
<data buffer [Size]>
<INDEXING MODE {AUTOSELECT | REBUILD | INCREMENTAL | DEFERRED]>
<ALLOW NO ACCESS | ALLOW READ ACCESS <USE [TempTSName]>>
<SET INTEGRITY PENDING CASCADE [IMMEDIATE | DEFERRED]>
```

The load command has numerous options, but most of the time you will only use a few of them. For example, there are options for where rejected data is to be stored, what kind of indexing is performed, what kind of access is allowed, and many others.

It is really important that you refer to the IBM Db2 manuals for more information on the load utility. This utility is very flexible and has so many options that if you attempt to use them without understanding what they are for, then you may become frustrated easily. The manuals contain numerous examples on how to use the load utility.

Restore Command

The RESTORE DATABASE command restores a database that has been backed up using the Db2 backup utility. The restored database is in the same state that it was in when the backup copy was made. The RESTORE DATABASE command can also be used to encrypt an existing database.

The **restore** utility can perform a number of services including overwriting an existing database, restoring backup images created by the backup utility, enabling a rollforward of the database if necessary, restoring incremental images (delta images), and other capabilities.

If you are restoring from one environment to another, new incremental or delta backups may be restricted until a full backup has been performed. A restore operation within the same environment utilizes the existing tablespaces and tablespace map.

A restore operation that is run against a new database reacquires all containers (even those that do not exist yet) and rebuilds an optimized tablespace map. A restore operation that is run over an existing database with one or more missing containers also reacquires all containers and rebuilds an optimized tablespace map.

The restore command is also the bookend to the backup command. It can restore a backup file(s) so that the database is returned to a previous known state. It is recommended that the restore command be tested prior to depending on it to protect your production data.

Command Syntax

```
RESTORE [DATABASE | DB] [databaseAlias]
  [User [username] [Using [password]]]
  [REBUILD WITH [TABLESPACE ([Tbspname])] |
  [ALL TABLRSPACES IN [DATABASE | IMAGE]]
  [EXCEPT TABLESPACE ([TbspName])]]
  [TABLESPACE ([TbspName]) [ONLINE] |
  HISTORY FILE [ONLINE]] |
  LOGS [ONLINE]]
  [INCREMENTAL [AUTO | AUTOMATIC | ABORT]]
  [FROM [SourceLocation] | USE TSM [OPTIONS [TSMOptions]]]
  [TAKEN AT {Timestamp]]
  [TO [TargetLocations]]
  [DBPATH ON [TargetPath]]
  [TRANSPORT [ STAGE IN StagingAlias] [USING STOGROUP StoGroupName]]
  [INTO [TargetAlias]] [LOGTARGET [LogLocation]]
  [NEWLOGPATH [LogsLocation]]
  [WITH [NumBuffers] BUFFERS]
  [BUFFER [BufferSize]]
  [REPLACE HISTORY FILE]
  [REPLACE EXISTING]
  [REDIRECT [GENERATE SCRIPT [ScriptFile]]]
  [PARALLELISM pParallelNum]]
  [WITHOUT ROLLING FORWARD]
  [WITHOUT PROMPTING]
```

The restore command has numerous options to choose from. In order to use it effectively, you should reference the IBM Db2 manuals for a complete understanding of just how this utility works.

Summary

This chapter has covered only a subset of the Db2 command utilities. There are many more available commands documented in the Db2 online documentation. The utilities covered here are the most used by administrators in their everyday tasks but are also useful to programmers. Be sure to refer to the proper online documentation for a full set of instructions for each command before trying to use it.

CHAPTER 6

Business Rules and Constraints

Creating business rules and constraints on your SQL tables is actually a part of the database design phase. We treat it as a separate topic as these rules can be added later instead of creating them at the same time as the tables. This is really a good thing as none of us can think of everything during the design phase.

There are two kinds of business rules and constraints – those that perform referential integrity of the tables and those that apply actual business rules. These two kinds of constraints are sometimes confused, but we will try to keep them separate in our explanation.

This chapter will group the constraints by their type. This will include indexes, NOT NULL attribute, primary keys, foreign keys, table checks, and informational constraints. In many cases, a constraint can fit into more than one category, which is why we will group them by Db2 type rather than by their constraint type.

NOT NULL Attribute

When you create a table in Db2, all columns in the table allow NULLs by default. If NULLs should not be allowed, you must explicitly include the NOT NULL phrase in the column definition. Consider the following table definition:

```
CREATE TABLE employee (
    emp_num CHAR(10) NOT NULL,
    name CHAR(50),
    location VARCHAR(30),
    create_date TIMESTAMP
    );
```

© W. David Ashley 2021
W. D. Ashley, *Foundation Db2 and Python*, https://doi.org/10.1007/978-1-4842-6942-8_6

In this table, the emp_num column must contain data, even if it is just a single blank. The NOT NULL constraint ensures that the column always has some data in it. It may not necessarily be valid data (we will discuss this topic later), but it must contain data of some type.

The columns name, location, and create_date may all have the NULL type assigned to them. This is the default for all columns that do not include the NOT NULL phrase as a part of the column definition.

If you need to add a NOT NULL phrase to a column definition, you can do that with the ALTER TABLE statement:

```
ALTER TABLE employee ALTER name CHAR(50) NOT NULL;
```

This will add the NOT NULL clause to the name column without modifying the data type.

Primary Key

A primary key identifies a column that uniquely identifies a single row in the table. You can assign a primary key column to a table using the PRIMARY KEY phrase. For instance, we could have added this phrase to the column definition to make the emp_num column the primary key:

```
emp_num CHAR(10) NOT NULL PRIMARY KEY,
```

You can also alter the table later to add this constraint:

```
ALTER TABLE employee ADD PRIMARY KEY (emp_num);
```

If the data in a table has no natural column that can act as a primary key, you can artificially create one for the table. Consider the following table definition:

```
CREATE TABLE employee (
    emp_num INTEGER NOT NULL PRIMARY KEY
    name CHAR(50),
    location VARCHAR(30),
    create_date TIMESTAMP
    );
```

Here we have modified the emp_num column so that Db2 will add one to the highest existing integer in the entire column and assign that to the new emp_num column automatically when a new row is inserted into the table.

You should not think of the primary key as a unique index even though that is what is created underneath. While they have many of the same characteristics, they are not the same. For one thing, a table can have only one primary key, but it can have many unique and nonunique indexes.

Indexes

A table can have many indexes, but usually has only one or two as indexing everything in a table is counterproductive. There are two kinds of indexes:

- Unique indexes: This type of index prevents an entry in the indexed column from appearing more than once in the table. The UNIQUE keyword specifies this kind of index.

- Nonunique indexes: This type of index will improve the ability of Db2 to read the table when it is used in the WHERE clause of a SELECT statement.

Indexes can be created when the CREATE INDEX statement is executed. The following example shows how to create an index on a column with the CREATE INDEX statement:

```
CREATE INDEX myindex ON employee (location);
```

An index can also be dropped with the DROP INDEX statement.

A word of warning is needed for indexes at this point. Try not to go overboard when creating indexes. You may think that indexing all columns in a table will give you the best access times for all your queries. This is completely untrue and will instead cause most of the indexes to be ignored.

Foreign Keys

Foreign keys are column values that refer to another column in a different table. This is done to ensure that that all foreign key values exist in the main table. For instance, when you assign a person to a department, you may want to ensure that the department actually exists before the operation can succeed. The following example will demonstrate this principle:

```
CREATE TABLE department (
    dept_num INTEGER NOT NULL PRIMARY KEY,
    name CHAR(50)
    );

CREATE TABLE employee (
    emp_num INTEGER NOT NULL PRIMARY KEY
    name CHAR(50),
    dept INTEGER REFERENCES department (dept_num),
    location VARCHAR(30),
    create_date TIMESTAMP
    );
```

The department table defines all departments within the organization. The employee table has a dept column that references the dept_num column in the department table. What this means is that when you try to insert a new record in the employee table, the system will check to make sure that the dept column value exists in the dept_num column in the department table. If no corresponding department number is found in the department table, then the INSERT will fail.

Foreign keys are a type of referential constraint, or sometimes known as a foreign key constraint. A foreign key can refer to either a primary key or an index. In the case of an index, the index must be a single column, but it does not need to be a unique index.

The following example shows a foreign key pointing to an index:

```
CREATE TABLE department (
    dept_num INTEGER NOT NULL,
    name CHAR(50)
    );

CREATE UNIQUE INDEX ON department (dept_num);
```

```
CREATE TABLE employee (
    emp_num INTEGER NOT NULL PRIMARY KEY
    name CHAR(50),
    dept INTEGER REFERENCES department (dept_num),
    location VARCHAR(30),
    create_date TIMESTAMP
    );
```

In the preceding example, the UNIQUE keyword ensures that all dept_num numbers are unique in the department table. An attempt to insert a duplicate department number in the table will be rejected.

CHECK and Unique Constraints

The CHECK constraint ensures that only values in a certain range are allowed to be in a table column. The following shows an example of a CHECK constraint:

```
CREATE TABLE employee (
    empid INTEGER,
    name VARCHAR(30),
    ssn VARCHAR(11) NOT NULL,
    salary INTEGER CHECK (salary >= 5000),
    job VARCHAR(10) CHECK (job IN ('Engineer', 'Sales', 'Manager')));
```

The salary column must have a value greater than or equal to 5000 when a row is inserted into or updated in the table. The job column must have one of the three values specified (case sensitive). The constraint expression can have the values as specified previously, or it could be a sub–SELECT statement that returns the set of specified valid values.

DEFAULT Constraint

The DEFAULT constraint allows you to specify a default value to a column when a row is written into the table. You specify a DEFAULT constraint as shown in the following example:

```
CREATE TABLE employee (
    empid INTEGER,
    name VARCHAR(30),
    ssn VARCHAR(11) WITH DEFAULT '999-99-999');
```

The following example INSERT statement will show how this constraint works:

```
INSERT INTO employee (empid, name)
    VALUES (005, 'Smith, James');
```

Note that the ssn field is not referenced. Normally this could cause a problem with the INSERT statement. But in this case, a default value for ssn has been specified, so no error is raised.

Triggers

Triggers are database objects that respond to events such as an INSERT, UPDATE, or DELETE on a specific table or view. Triggers can be used in addition to all the other referential constraints or CHECK restraints to enforce data integrity business rules. There are five components associated with any trigger:

- The subject on which the trigger is defined – tables or views

- The event that initiates the trigger – an INSERT, UPDATE, or DELETE action

- The activation time of the trigger – a BEFORE or AFTER event

- The granularity that specifies whether the trigger's actions are performed once for the table or once for each of the affected rows – a FOR EACH STATEMENT or FOR EACH ROW action

- The action that the trigger performs – one or more of the following elements:

  a. CALL statement

  b. DECLARE and/or SET statement

  c. WHILE and/or FOR loop

  d. IF, SIGNAL, ITERATE, LEAVE, and GET DIAGNOSTIC statements

  e. SELECT statement

  f. INSERT, UPDATE, DELETE, and MERGE SQL statements (only for AFTER and INSTEAD OF triggers)

Triggers are classified as BEFORE, AFTER, and INSTEAD OF:

- **BEFORE** triggers are activated before an UPDATE or INSERT operation, and the values that are being updated or inserted can be changed before the database is modified.

- **AFTER** triggers are activated after an INSERT, UPDATE, or DELETE operation and are used to maintain relationships between data or keep audit trail information.

- **INSTEAD OF** triggers define how to perform an INSERT, UPDATE, or DELETE operation on a view where these operations are otherwise not allowed.

The syntax for creating a trigger is as follows:

```
CREATE or REPLACE TRIGGER [Triggername]
    <NO CASCADE> | <AFTER | BEFORE | INSTEAD OF> [TriggerEvent]
    ON [Tablename | ViewName]
    REFERENCING <OLD AS | NEW AS | OLD TABLE AS | NEW TABLE AS>
    [CorrelationName | Identifier]
    <FOR EACH ROW | FOR EACH STATEMENT>
    <Action>
```

where

- TriggerName: Identifies the name to assign to the trigger to be created.

- TriggerEvent: Specifies the triggered action associated with the trigger to be executed whenever one of the events is applied to the subject table or subject view.

- TableName: Identifies the name of the table (the subject) on which the trigger is defined.

- ViewName: Identifies the name of the view (the subject) on which the trigger is defined.

- CorrelationName: A temporary table name that identifies the row state before triggering the SQL operation.

- Identifier: A temporary table name that identifies the set of affected rows before triggering the SQL operation.

- Action: Specifies the action to perform when a trigger is activated. A trigger action is composed of an SQL procedure statement and an optional condition for the execution of the SQL procedure statement.

While there are almost an infinite number of ways to use triggers, we will show only four simple examples. These examples can be used as the basis for other triggers you create.

The following example illustrates a BEFORE trigger that is activated when an INSERT statement is executed on the employee table. The trigger assigns a value of the next day when it detects a NULL being inserted into the empstart column of the employee table:

```
CREATE OR REPLACE TRIGGER employeeJoinDate
    NO CASCADE BEFORE INSERT ON enployee
    REFERENCING NEW AS N
    FOR EACH ROW
    MODE DB2SQL
    WHEN (N.empstartdate IS NULL)
    SET N.empstartdate = CURRENT DATE + 1 DAY;
```

In the following example, an AFTER trigger is activated when an INSERT statement is executed on the employee table. If the row being inserted into the employee table is due to a new hire, the trigger statement will update the employee head count in the company statistics table company_stats:

```
CREATE OR REPLACE TRIGGER employeeNewHire
    NO CASCADE AFTER INSERT ON employee
    FOR EACH ROW
    MODE DB2SQL
    UPDATE company_stats SET emp_tcount = emp_tcount + 1;
```

What if an HR department wants to check for an employee's pay raise before the salary change is made in the employee table? For any employee, if the pay raise is double the current salary, it must be recorded in the salary_audit table for analysis purposes. An AFTER trigger can be created to insert the appropriate data in the salary_audit table:

```
CREATE OR REPLACE TRIGGER employeeSalaryUpdate
    AFTER UPDATE OF salary ON employee
    REFERENCING NEW AS N OLD AS O
    FOR EACH ROW
    MODE DB2SQL
    WHEN (N.salary > O.salary * 2)
      INSERT INTO salary_audit
        (empno, old_salary, New_salary, rating)
        VALUES (N.empid, O.salary, N.salary, N.rating);
```

Triggers can also be used to raise errors through the SIGNAL statement and to prevent specific operations on the tables. If there is a rule that no pay raise can exceed 300%, you can create a trigger that will check for this condition:

```
CREATE TRIGGER salaryRaiseLimit
    AFTER UPDATE OF salary ON employee
    REFERENCING NEW AS N OLD AS O
    FOR EACH ROW
    WHEN (N.salary > O.salary * 3)
    SIGNAL SQLSTATE '75000'  SET MESSAGE_TEXT = 'Salary increase > 300%';
```

Summary

In this chapter, we have introduced the concept of business rules and constraints. These rules and constraints can help you implement the rules your organization may have established for the upkeep of their data. They can also help implement organizational characteristics for the organization as well as establish relationships between different sections of the company.

## CHAPTER 7

Writing Good SQL for Db2

Writing good SQL is really about database performance. Although tuning of the database can help with performance, bad SQL will impact performance in ways that tuning the database just cannot cure. When the database administrator(s) has done their job, it is time for the training of the users to begin. All relational databases have their quirks, and it is paramount for the users to be aware of these and have the knowledge to either bypass them or create SQL that takes advantage of the database design and features.

Db2 is designed to hold and process huge amounts of data. Because of that, many of the design goals and features are quite different from other relational databases. The SQL optimizer is one of the most sophisticated in the industry. Database data can be spread over a wide variety of devices and an array of computational entities. All of this power does not come without some cost, and this chapter concerns the design and use of SQL.

This chapter will address some simple ways to structure your SQL to take advantage of the Db2 design. It will cover a variety of areas so that you have a good understanding of how Db2 works and what you can do to make your SQL perform better.

Relational Theory

Relational databases are designed around the mathematical theory of sets. Set theory is a very old and understood theory of relationships between entities or, in our case, data. All relational databases have set theory at their heart.

Because of this design, the storage of data in the database has practically no resemblance to traditional file systems. This makes it really hard for both programmers and users to understand why you should not do things in the traditional way. The very first thing to teach new users is that doing things in the traditional ways will ALWAYS cause detrimental impacts on database performance. And in some cases, the performance will be worse than sequentially accessing a file for the same data.

© W. David Ashley 2021
W. D. Ashley, *Foundation Db2 and Python*, https://doi.org/10.1007/978-1-4842-6942-8_7

Relational databases have a tremendous amount of power built into them. When working with Db2, you should always try to make use of that power mainly because it will almost always be better than trying to design your own solution.

One of the mistakes that new users make is thinking of a database table as a file. They are not files, and even the data in a table row is not stored together. The reason for this goes back to the set theory of design. It will always be easier to structure data on the fly rather than by breaking structured data apart and restructuring it as a result set.

The next mistake new users make is thinking that construction of a result set happens a little at a time. This is a big mistake. When the first result row is presented to the user, the complete result set has already been completed by the system. Thus, processing the result set a line at a time delays the destruction of the result set and uses up valuable system scratch space.

These are the two really big problems for new users and programmers, but another mistake made especially by programmers involves processing the data to produce a new result after fetching the data. New programmers sometimes assume that the database system is inefficient in dynamically modifying a result – like adding a fixed numerical value to a result column. This is just not the case. The database system is much faster at this sort of calculation than any program could be.

New users are also sometimes afraid of creating SQL that is complex, thinking that the system will find it hard to interpret for a valid result. The SQL optimizer for Db2 is very efficient at breaking apart the input SQL and efficiently interpreting and executing it.

The last mistake users make is to code SQL to ask for data you already know. For instance, if you ask for data on Dept. 4, do not ask for the department number as a part of the result set. This is just a waste of time and resources.

The last thing to cover is the data types used in Db2 and contrasting them to the native data types of the hardware systems. For instance, very few smaller systems natively support decimal data. Sometimes there are libraries available that can process this data, but even then, it will require some programming to accommodate the decimal data.

Reduce Passes Through Data

One of the easiest ways to reduce the processing of SQL queries is to eliminate multiple passes through the same data. For instance, if you are looking for employees whose salaries are out of range, you might create two queries to return the data:

```
SELECT firstnme, midinit, empno
   FROM emp
   WHERE salary > 75000;
```

```
SELECT firstnme, midinit, empno
   FROM emp
   WHERE salary < 10000;
```

These two queries will return the employees whose salaries are either above the salary range or below it. If the number of employees is really large, each query will take some time to process. The problem here is the question we really want answered is what "employees are out of range." This fundamental question can be answered with a single query:

```
SELECT firstnme, midinit, empno
   FROM emp
   WHERE salary > 75000 OR salary < 10000;
```

This query will make a single pass through the data to list all the employees that are either above or below the range.

It is really important to always step back from a question when it takes two queries to obtain the data. Try to figure out the fundamental question you are asking as that usually leads to a single query that really answers your question.

The following shows another example of how multiple passes can creep into your SQL coding:

```
SELECT creator, name, 'Table '
   FROM sysibm.systables
   WHERE type = 'T'
UNION
SELECT creator, name, 'View  '
   FROM sysibm.systables
   WHERE type = 'V'
UNION
SELECT creator, name, 'Alias '
   FROM sysibm.systables
   WHERE type = 'A'
UNION
```

```
SELECT creator, name, 'Global'
   FROM sysibm.systables
   WHERE type = 'G'
ORDER BY creator, name;
```

This simple statement causes four passes through the `sysibm.systables` table. The result output shows all the table-like objects in the database catalog. However, the statement can be simplified so that only a single pass is necessary over the `sysibm.systables` table.

When joining two or more tables, it will be very useful for the WHERE clause to refer to an indexed column in each table you reference. All of this is to prevent a complete table scan looking for the proper rows in each table:

```
SELECT creator, name,
   CASE type
      WHEN 'T' THEN 'Table '
      WHEN 'V' THEN 'View  '
      WHEN 'A' THEN "Alias '
      WHEN 'G' THEN 'Global'
   END
   FROM sysibm.systables
   ORDER BY creator, name;
```

This new query provides the same results as the previous one but only requires a single pass through the `sysibm.systables` table. It is also much easier to read and understand.

The following shows how you can make mass updates with only a single pass through a table:

```
UPDATE emp
SET salary = CASE workdept
      WHEN 'A01' THEN salary * .04
      WHEN 'C01' THEN salary * .02
      WHEN 'D11' THEN salary * .10
      WHEN 'D21' THEN salary * .50
      ELSE salary * .01
   WHERE edlevel > 15;
```

Using Indexes to Increase Performance

When querying data from the database, it is really important to utilize indexes wherever possible. The increase in performance can be quite dramatic. You do NOT need to necessarily fetch columns that have an index on them, but instead try to utilize them wherever possible in the SQL WHERE clause. For instance, if the empno column has an index on it, you should attempt to utilize the index in your queries:

```
SELECT firstnme, midinit, lastnme, dept
   FROM emp
   WHERE empno > 10000
```

The preceding statement will now utilize the index to locate the employee row(s) without a full table scan. The column empno has an index on it; thus, Db2 can use it to locate the rows to be returned. Note that it is not necessary to retrieve the indexed column to utilize its index. A reference in the WHERE clause is sufficient to prevent a full table scan.

Also, you should be aware that Db2 can create an index on the fly to help query a table or tables. For instance, the following WHERE clause will cause dynamic indexes to be created on the salary, bonus, and comm columns to help reduce the access time for the data:

```
SELECT empno, firstnme, lastnme
FROM emp
WHERE salary + bonus + comm > 100000.00;
```

The indexes that are created are only temporary and will be deleted when the query is complete.

Sorting and Grouping

Sorting is sometimes a confusing topic for new SQL users because there are some underlying rules that govern it. Also, sorting can be invoked by the ORDER BY clause or by the DISTINCT keyword on the SELECT clause.

One aspect of the ORDER BY clause is that the column(s) named in that clause does NOT have to be retrieved in the output (appears after the SELECT keyword). Many new users are always surprised by that aspect of ordering the output data. An example is shown here:

```
SELECT empno, lastnme, firstnme
FROM emp
ORDER BY workdept;
```

As you can see, the `workdept` does not appear in the output, but the data will be ordered by that value.

You should also limit the number of columns to be sorted. The more columns you include, the longer the sort will take.

The DISTINCT keyword always causes a sort, even if there are no duplicate rows. You should be very careful when using DISTINCT as the overhead for it can be high. However, this is not a recommendation to never use it as there may be very valid reasons for doing so.

Grouping with SQL can be extremely helpful when you want to return aggregate data. Consider the following query:

```
SELECT workdept, SUM(salary)
   FROM emp
   GROUP BY workdept;
```

This causes the output to contain a single line for each `workdept` along with the aggregate sum of salaries for all the employees in the `workdept`. The order of the `workdept`s will be random since no ORDER BY clause was used. Additionally, the HAVING clause can eliminate departments that are of no use to you:

```
SELECT workdept, SUM(salary)
   FROM emp
   GROUP BY workdept
   HAVING AVG(salary) < 15000;
```

Programs Containing SQL

Programs that contain SQL are sometimes called "black box code" because the SQL is hidden from view by the users that run the programs. These programs are created by programmers who work from a set of requirements created by their users. Problems arise when the programmer(s) takes shortcuts when writing the SQL for the program. Let us look at an example that will make the SQL inefficient, and thus the program will be inefficient.

If the program requires three different kinds of data from the `customer` table, the best way to do this is to write three different queries against the `customer` table:

```
SELECT firstnme, lastnme, address, city, state, zipcode
   FROM customer
   WHERE areacode = :HV-AC;
```

```
SELECT custid, firstnme, lastnme, phoneno
   FROM customer
   WHERE areacode = :HV-AC;

SELECT custid, firstnme, lastnme, custtype
   FROM customer
   WHERE areacode = :HV-AC;
```

All of the preceding queries are very efficient and require very few resources from the database. But, in the name of reduced programming effort, the programmer(s) may decide to code them as follows to reduce the number of SQL statements in the program:

```
SELECT custid, firstnme, lastnme, address, city, state, zipcode, phonno,
custtype
   FROM customer
   WHERE areacode = :HV-AC;
```

This is not nearly as efficient as the three previous queries. It is also bad form because it will always return columns in which the users are uninterested. The bottom line is this is a terrible idea. While it may seem to be saving programmer time, it wastes user time and database resources every time the query is run.

Use Db2 Utilities Where Possible

Programmers and users alike should always investigate the possibilities of using a Db2 utility in place of a custom-made program. In most cases, the Db2 utility will be much more efficient than a programmer-created program. The vast majority of utilities in Db2 have existed for decades and have 99% of all bugs already removed. Plus, the efficiency of these utilities has been honed over the years, far longer than any other locally created program.

The load and import utilities can be used to add or replace data in existing tables. These utilities are very efficient, especially the load utility. They can also deal with very large input data sets. There are any number of options supported by these utilities that can modify how the data is loaded into a table including skipping some input data.

The unload utility can extract data from a table in mass amounts very quickly. It uses an SQL statement to determine the data to be unloaded and thus is easily modified by users to match their requirements.

The MERGE SQL statement, while not a Db2 utility, is another way to take data from two tables and merge it into a single table. It is a very powerful SQL statement with a number of options for matching the data to be merged.

The TRUNCATE SQL statement is another tool that is not a Db2 utility. This one statement can remove all the data in a table and optionally reclaim the storage space occupied by the table.

Db2 Functions

The Db2 system provides a large collection of built-in functions (BIFs) that can be used in your SQL statements that can improve the retrieval of the exact data you are looking for. These functions are as much a part of SQL and the Db2 optimizer as the SQL statements themselves. Using them in your SQL statements usually does not cause performance issues.

From a broad perspective, there are two types of functions provided by Db2. There are the built-in functions that are supplied by the database and user-developed functions that are supplied by users and programmers. The built-in functions are very efficient and can be used by anyone developing a SQL statement for Db2. The user-defined functions must be developed, usually by programmers, in order to be available for SQL statements.

There are many types of BIFs, a few of which are listed here:

- Aggregate functions: These are used to compute summary information from a column contained in one or more rows and summarize it in some form.

- Scalar functions: These functions return a subset of column data in a single row.

- Table functions: These functions return a set of columns from within the WHERE clause.

- Row functions: These are not available yet in Db2 for LUW.

The current Db2 BIFs are listed here:

ABS: Returns the absolute value of a column from a set of rows.

AVG: Computes the average of a set of column values.

CEILING: Returns the smallest integer value greater than or equal to the argument.

CHAR: Returns a fixed-length character string of the argument.

COALESCE: Returns the value of the first non-NULL expression.

CONCAT: Returns the concatenation of two compatible string arguments.

CORRELATION: An expression that returns a value of any built-in numeric data type.

COUNT: Counts the number of rows in a column result.

COVARIANCE: Returns the population (covariance) of a set of number pairs.

DATE: Returns the Db2 date derived from an expression.

IDENTITY_VAL_LOCAL: Returns the most recently assigned value for an identity element.

INT: Returns an integer for a number or a character string representation of an integer.

LENGTH: Returns the length of a value.

LOCATE: Returns the position where the first occurrence of an argument starts within another argument.

LOWER: Returns the argument string in lowercase.

LPAD: Returns a padded string argument on the left with blanks (or another string).

LTRIM: Returns a string with bytes removed from the left of the string.

MAX: Returns the maximum value in a column from a set of rows.

MIN: Returns the minimum value in a column from a set of rows.

POSITION: Returns the position of the first occurrence of an argument within another argument.

RAND: Returns a random floating-point number between 0 and 1.

REPLACE: Returns a string with all occurrences of a string with another string.

ROUND: Returns a number rounded to the specified number of digits to the right or left of the decimal point.

RPAD: Returns a padded string argument on the right with blanks (or another string).

RTRIM: Returns a string with bytes removed from the right of the string.

SQRT: Returns the square root of the argument.

STDDEV: Returns the standard deviation in a column from a set of rows.

SUBSTR: Returns a substring of a string argument.

SUM: Returns the sum of all columns from a set of rows.

UPPER: Returns the argument string in uppercase.

UNNEST: Returns a result table that includes a row for each element of an array.

VARIANCE: Returns the variance of all columns from a set of rows.

Multiple Ways to Code SQL

With SQL, just like any other language, there is more than one way to obtain the results you are looking for from a query. Examine the following statement:

```
SELECT empno, lastname
    FROM emp
    WHERE workdept LIKE 'A%';
```

While that may get the result you are looking for, it may return a far greater set of rows than you are expecting. The preceding statement assumes you know that there are only three departments starting with the letter "A." But in the future, there may be far more departments that start with that letter. A better alternative is to code what you know to prevent problems in the future and to improve efficiency:

```
SELECT empno, lastname
    FROM emp
    WHERE workdept IN('A00', 'A01', 'A02');
```

This will at least give you correctly targeted results, but it will improve performance as well.

Summary

This chapter has introduced several individual topics all designed to help you write good SQL for the Db2 database. Good SQL is defined as efficient, logical, and easy to read. The result of writing good SQL is that it is easily understood and easy to maintain.

## CHAPTER 8

Python and ibm_db

In order to access Db2 from Python, you will need to download and set up the ibm_db module. Currently, this module is not available through any Linux, Unix, or Windows code repositories. However, it can be installed through the Python pip system or downloaded as source and compiled on your system. We highly recommend that you use pip to install the ibm_db module. But before you install it, there are some prerequisites that need to be in place before you can successfully perform the install:

1. Your system must be capable of compiling the source code. The C compiler and linker must be installed in order to create the module. On Linux you can check that the compiler is installed by running the following command:

   ```
   gcc -v
   ```

2. If pip is not installed, then install it using your distribution's package installer. Do not be concerned about Python versions of pip as the install will create a link to the proper version of pip for your version of Python:

   ```
   sudo dnf install pip
   ```

   or

   ```
   sudo yum install pip
   ```

3. If you are running on Linux or Unix, the python-devel package must be installed. Use your distribution's package installer to install the python-devel (or python3-devel) package:

   ```
   sudo dnf install python-devel
   ```

   or

   ```
   sudo yum install python-devel
   ```

© W. David Ashley 2021
W. D. Ashley, *Foundation Db2 and Python*, https://doi.org/10.1007/978-1-4842-6942-8_8

Once you have the perquisites installed, you can install the ibm_db package:

```
sudo pip install ibm_db
```

or

```
sudo python3 pip3 install ibm_db              (for RHEL or CentOS)
```

This will install the Db2 package so that it will be available to your Python scripts. You do not need to install the Db2 client software unless you need it for other purposes. The ibm_db module will allow a Python script/program to access Db2 either locally or remotely without any other software packages.

The ibm_db package contains two modules that can be imported into your scripts: the ibm_db module, which is the standard way to access Db2 from Python, and the ibm_db_dbi module, which conforms to the Python DB-API 2.0 standard for accessing database systems generically. In this book, we will concentrate on the ibm_db module because that module is the base module for accessing Db2 and is actually used by the ibm_db_dbi module to perform all the work to access Db2.

The ibm_db module is a C source code–based module. It is open source and can be found at http://github.com/ibmdb/python-ibmdb/. Also, the Python tests for the module are available at the same location as well as the Python source code for the ibm_db_dbi module.

If you get error messages when you try to install the ibm_db package, then one or more of the prerequisites are not installed. If the message claims the Python.h file cannot be found, then you have not installed the python-devel package from the Linux/Unix distribution's code repository, or it is not installed properly.

Once the ibm_db package is successfully installed, you are ready to write your first Python script to access Db2.

What follows are some examples of using the ibm_db module to retrieve data from the sample database. All these examples prompt you for a username and password. These values are always those that exist on the Db2 server, not on your local machine (unless that is where the Db2 system resides). If the sample database was installed on the server with the default options, then the username will be db2inst1, and the password will be whatever was set by the database administrator.

Your First Python ibm_db Program

The sample Python code in this chapter accesses the sample database, which comes with Db2. You will need to install the sample database or have your Db2 administrator install it for you. If you are installing it yourself on your own system, there is only one command you need to run to get it installed. Be sure to run this command as the db2inst1 account:

```
db2sampl -force -sql
```

This will take a little time to install, so be patient. Once installed, you can run the following commands to test that the database has been successfully installed:

```
db2 connect to sample
db2 "select * from department"
```

This should display the department table, and it should contain 14 records.

Once this executes successfully, you are now ready to write your first Python programs that access the Db2 sample database.

Our first Python program/script is actually very simple. It emulates the SQL select command we used previously to test the sample database. We want a nicely formatted display of the table contents, and we want to perform all the error checking needed to make sure we can track any errors the program may encounter. This will require a rather longer program than a first example usually requires, but it also gives us a chance to describe a number of ibm_db APIs that you will be using in all your Python programs.

The first Python example program follows in Listing 8-1.

Listing 8-1. Display the department Table

```python
#!/usr/bin/python

import sys, getpass
import ibm_db

def getColNamesWidths(results):
    # get the width of each column
    columns = list()
    col = 0
    numColumns = 0
    try:
```

```
        numColumns = ibm_db.num_fields(results)
    except Exception:
        pass
    # If information about the number columns returned could not be obtained,
    # display an error message and exit .
    if numColumns is False:
        print("\nERROR: Unable to obtain information about the result set
        produced.")
        conn.closeConnection()
        exit(-1)
    while col < numColumns:
        col_name = ibm_db.field_name(results, col)
        col_width = ibm_db.field_width(results, col)
        # the field name can be bigger than the display width
        col_width = max(len(col_name), col_width)
        columns.append((col_name, col_width))
        col += 1
    return columns # return a list of tuples (name, size)

def populateColTitleLines(columns):
    # populate the two title lines for the results
    col = 0
    line = ''
    lines = []
    # do the title line
    while col < len(columns):
        (col_name, col_width) = columns[col]
        title = col_name + ((col_width - len(col_name)) * ' ')
        line += '  ' + title
        col += 1
    lines.append(line)
    # do the underlines
    col = 0
    line = ''
    while col < len(columns):
        (col_name, col_width) = columns[col]
```

```python
        line += '   ' + (col_width * '-')
        col += 1
    lines.append(line)
    return lines # return the two title lines

def populateLines(results, headerLines):
    # print the data records
    lines = []
    record = ibm_db.fetch_tuple(results)
    while record is not False:
        line = ''
        col = 0
        numColumns = 0
        try:
            numColumns = ibm_db.num_fields(results)
        except Exception:
            pass
        # If information about the number columns returned could not be
          obtained,
        # display an error message and exit .
        if numColumns is False:
            print("\nERROR: Unable to obtain information about the result
            set produced.")
            conn.closeConnection()
            exit(-1)
        while col < numColumns:
            colstr = record[col]
            (name, col_width) = headerLines[col]
            coltype = ibm_db.field_type(results, col)
            if record[col] is None:
                line += '   -' + ((col_width - 1) * ' ')
            elif coltype in ("clob", "dbclob", "blob", "xml", "string"):
                # these are the string types
                line += '   ' + str(colstr) + ((col_width - len(colstr)) * ' ')
```

```
            else:
                # these are the numeric types, or at least close enough
                colstr = str(colstr)
                line += '  ' + ((col_width - len(colstr)) * ' ') + colstr
            col += 1
        lines.append(line)
        record = ibm_db.fetch_tuple(results)
    return lines

# main program
driver = "{IBM DB2 ODBC DRIVER}"  # Db2 driver information
host = '192.168.1.201'            # database host IP or dns address
port = "50000"                    # host port
db = "sample"                     # database registered name
uid = None                        # userid on the database host
pw = None                         # password of the uid
autocommit = ''                   # autocommit default override
connecttype = ''                  # connect type default override
uid = input("Enter the Db2 userid to be used: ")
pw = getpass.getpass(prompt = "Password for %s: " % uid)
if pw == None or pw == '':
    print("The password you entered is incorrect.")
    exit(-1)
conn_str = 'DRIVER=' + driver + ';HOSTNAME=' + host + \
           ';PORT=' + port + ';DATABASE=' + db + \
           ';UID=' + uid + ';PWD=' + pw
connID = ibm_db.connect(conn_str, autocommit, connecttype)
# If the connection fails for any reason an uncaught exception is thrown
# and the program will exit with an error.

# get the records from the database
sqlstmt = 'select * from department'
try:
    results = ibm_db.exec_immediate(connID, sqlstmt)
except Exception:
    pass
```

```
# If the sql statement could not be executed, display an error message and exit
if results is False:
    print("\nERROR: Unable to execute the SQL statement specified.")
    ibm_db.close(connID)
    exit(-1)

# fetch SQL results and format lines
headerLines = getColNamesWidths(results)
titleLines = populateColTitleLines(headerLines)
dataLines = populateLines(results, headerLines)
selrecords = len(dataLines)

#print the result lines
for line in titleLines:
    print(line)
for line in dataLines:
    print(line)
# print the number of records returned
print('\n    ' + str(selrecords) + ' record(s) selected.')

ibm_db.close(connID)
exit(0)
```

The Python script starts with the usual first line to notify the system that this is a Python script and then specifies the Python interpreter to be executed.

The next two lines are the Python import statements that are needed by the script:

```
import sys, getpass
import ibm_db
```

The only thing here that is out of the ordinary is the import of the ibm_db module.

The first function, getColNamesWidths(), obtains the column name and display width needed for each column from the result table. The call to the ibm_db.num_fields() function obtains the number of columns that the result set contains. Once we have that number, we loop over each column and call the ibm_db.field_name() and ibm_db.field_width() to obtain the column name and the column display width. These values will be used to add a title to each column and set the column display width. These values are then returned to the caller.

The next function, populateColTitleLines(), creates two lines, which will be eventually printed to the screen. These lines are a column title line and a separator dashed line. It utilizes the values from the previous function getColNamesWidths() to figure out how to format these lines. Once the lines have been created, they are returned to the caller as a Python list.

The next function, populateLines(), creates the lines fetched from the department table and formats each record as a display line using information passed to the function. Each line created is added to a Python list and then returned to the caller. Each result set record is fetched via the ibm_db.fetch_tuple() function and then formatted from the information passed to the function.

The main program code immediately follows the populateLines() function. The first part of the main program code sets some values that will be used later when the program connects to the Db2 database. The driver variable is always the same in all your Python scripts that use the ibm_db module. The host variable is either the IP address or the DNS name of the server that holds the sample database. If the database is local on your machine, then it can also be the IP address 127.0.0.1. The db variable has the name of the database you want to connect to; in our case, this is sample. We leave the uid and pw variables uninitialized so we do not code the userid and password information into the program. The autocommit and connecttype variables are options that we are not using in this script.

The next lines obtain the uid and pw variable information from the user. We then call the ibm_db.connect() function to actually connect to Db2 and the database specified by the previous variables. If this function fails for any reason, the Python script will exit with an error message. This is a deliberate decision so that we do not have a lot of code built into the program to correct information supplied by the user or mistyped into the script.

The next two sections of code are where the real work is performed. The first section sets the SQL statement to be executed. In this case, we want to fetch all information about the department table. We then call ibm_db.exec_immediate() to execute the SQL statement. If the ibm_db.exec_immediate() failed, an error message will be displayed, and the program will exit with an error message. If it succeeds, we proceed to the next section of code.

The next section of code calls the three functions defined in our program to fetch and display the results of the SQL statement. These functions were described previously.

The last major section actually prints the column titles and the fetched data to the standard output.

The last section calls `ibm_db.close()` to close our session with the Db2 database and exit the script.

Whew! That was a lot of code, but it is important to note that we included all the necessary error checking and produced a nicely formatted report back to our program user. Also, this is code that can be used over and over again in almost any program you write that uses the `select` statement or as the basis for a much more complicated and bigger program. And that is exactly what we will do in our later examples. Most of the program will be reused without any changes, and only the SQL statement will be changed or code added to that section to support extended functionality.

The output of Listing 8-1 is provided in Listing 8-2.

Listing 8-2. Output of Listing 8-1

```
$ ./example8-1.py
Enter the Db2 userid to be used: db2inst1
Password for db2inst1:
  DEPTNO  DEPTNAME                         MGRNO   ADMRDEPT  LOCATION
  ------  -------------------------------  ------  --------  ---------
  A00     SPIFFY COMPUTER SERVICE DIV.     000010  A00       -
  B01     PLANNING                         000020  A00       -
  C01     INFORMATION CENTER               000030  A00       -
  D01     DEVELOPMENT CENTER               -       A00       -
  D11     MANUFACTURING SYSTEMS            000060  D01       -
  D21     ADMINISTRATION SYSTEMS           000070  D01       -
  E01     SUPPORT SERVICES                 000050  A00       -
  E11     OPERATIONS                       000090  E01       -
  E21     SOFTWARE SUPPORT                 000100  E01       -
  F22     BRANCH OFFICE F2                 -       E01       -
  G22     BRANCH OFFICE G2                 -       E01       -
  H22     BRANCH OFFICE H2                 -       E01       -
  I22     BRANCH OFFICE I2                 -       E01       -
  J22     BRANCH OFFICE J2                 -       E01       -

  14 record(s) selected.
```

Although there are some small differences between our output and the display from the test Db2 command from the beginning of the chapter, it is essentially the same. We deliberately spaced the columns with two spaces to better separate the columns visually. Records that contain NULL data have a single dash character to indicate the NULL value in the beginning character of the column.

At this point, we should point out that this book has an appendix devoted to documenting the ibm_db APIs. Although this information has been taken from the ibm_db documentation, we have added a few notes that we hope make the documentation clearer and enhance it to make your programs more readable.

Using Parameter Markers

Our next example is slightly more complicated. It uses what are known as parameter markers to allow dynamic substitution of Python variable information into an SQL statement. This means that the values for parameter markers come from outside the SQL statement. In order to make this work, we have to use some different ibm_db API calls to prepare the SQL statement, substitute the variables, and then execute the statement.

We will essentially be using the same code from our previous example, but one section of the code will be different. The modified code is shown in Listing 8-3.

Listing 8-3. The Modified Code

```
              .
              .
              .


# get the records from the database
sqlstmt = 'SELECT projname, deptno FROM project WHERE deptno = ?'
prepstmt = ibm_db.prepare(connID, sqlstmt)
if prepstmt is False:
    print("Unable to prepare the SQL statement.")
    exit(-1)
deptid = 'B01'
retcode = ibm_db.bind_param(prepstmt, 1, deptid, ibm_db.SQL_PARAM_INPUT, \
                        ibm_db.SQL_CHAR)
```

```
try:
    results = ibm_db.execute(prepstmt)
except Exception:
    pass
# If the sql statement could not be executed, display an error message and exit
if results is False:
    print("\nERROR: Unable to execute the SQL statement specified.")
    ibm_db.close(connID)
    exit(-1)
```

.
.
.

Remember, the code before this section and after it is the same as in Listing 8-1 with the exception of two Python statements, so be careful in recreating this code if you are not using the packaged code from Apress.

The SQL statement is pretty normal except for the last character in the statement. The question mark (?) identifies a parameter marker. This is where we will substitute a Python variable later in the code. An SQL statement can have as many parameter markers as you need and can contain data or even SQL keywords. In our case, it will contain the specific department number we are looking for.

The next line is a call to ibm_db.prepare(). This will parse the SQL statement and make note of any parameter markers. This must be done prior to substituting the data into the SQL statement. We then check the return code from ibm_db.prepare() to make sure it succeeded before we proceed.

The next statement sets the Python variable we will substitute into the SQL statement. Where this value comes from is entirely up to you. It could be an input parameter to the Python program, it could come from a file, or you could even prompt the user for the value. Just make sure you do the proper error checking to the value prior to using it.

The next statement calls ibm_db.bind_param() to bind the Python variable to the SQL statement. The first parameter to the function identifies the prepared statement output from the previous call to ibm_db.prepare(). The second parameter is the Python variable to be substituted (or bound) in the SQL statement. In this case, it is the department number to be used. We need this in case you have coded more than one parameter marker in the SQL statement. You will need a separate call to ibm_db.bind_ param() for each parameter marker. The third parameter specifies whether the marker is an input, output, or input/output variable. The fourth parameter specifies the SQL type of variable that is being passed.

The next set of statements surround our call to ibm_db.execute() for error checking purposes. This function actually executes the prepared SQL statement. The code that follows checks to make sure that the execution succeeded.

After executing the SQL statement, the code after is our calls to the three functions and then printing the results of the SQL statement. This code is unchanged from our previous example.

It is highly recommended that you read the documentation for the ibm_db.prepare() function. There are a large number of parameter types to identify the SQL data types that you should become familiar with.

SQL statements with parameter markers are probably the most used statement types in programs. They are highly flexible and require only a little more code to accommodate in your Python code.

Listing 8-4 provides the output from this example.

Listing 8-4. Output from Listing 8-3

```
$ ./example8-2.py
Enter the Db2 userid to be used: db2inst1
Password for db2inst1:
  PROJNAME                  DEPTNO
  ------------------------  ------
  WELD LINE PLANNING        B01
```

Our SQL statement only specified the retrieval of two columns, and there is only one department with the designation B01. The report is small because there is only one department with the number specified, but it gets to the point about how parameter markers can be very useful.

More on Parameter Markers

The next example uses multiple parameter markers to create a selection of values that are used to query the project table. Basically, we want to list all the project names that have specified department numbers.

Again, we will be using the basic code from the first example in this project to produce the report while only showing the modified code (Listing 8-5).

Listing 8-5. Using Multiple Parameter Values

.

.

.

```
# get the records from the database
sqlstmt = 'SELECT projname, deptno FROM project WHERE deptno = ? OR deptno = ?'
prepstmt = ibm_db.prepare(connID, sqlstmt)
if prepstmt is False:
    print("Unable to prepare the statement.")
    exit(-1)
deptid1 = 'B01'
deptid2 = 'D01'
retcode = ibm_db.bind_param(prepstmt, 1, deptid1, ibm_db.SQL_PARAM_INPUT, \
                        ibm_db.SQL_CHAR)
retcode = ibm_db.bind_param(prepstmt, 2, deptid2, ibm_db.SQL_PARAM_INPUT, \
                        ibm_db.SQL_CHAR)
results = ibm_db.execute(prepstmt)
```

.

.

.

Remember, the code before this section and after it is the same as in Listing 8-1 with the exception of two Python statements, so be careful in recreating this code if you are not using the packaged code from Apress.

The select statement for this query contains two parameter values. The first marker will be labeled as 1; the second is labeled as 2. Parameter markers are always labeled from left to right in the SQL statement.

Next, we prepare the SQL statement with a call to ibm_db.prepare() just as all SQL statements with parameter markers need to be. If the call returns False, then we produce an error message and exit the Python program.

The assignments to Python variables that will be substituted into the parameter markers are next in the listing. Again, these can come from anywhere. We assign with them values here just to make what is happening as clear as possible.

Now we call ibm_db.bind_param() twice, once for each parameter marker. Once the value is bound to the SQL prepared statement, it remains bound until another call to ibm_cb.bind_param() is made.

Finally, we call ibm_db.execute() to obtain the query result.

Listing 8-6 shows the output of this query.

Listing 8-6. Output from Listing 8-5

```
$ ../examples/example8-3.py
Enter the Db2 userid to be used: db2inst1
Password for db2inst1:
    PROJNAME                    DEPTNO
    -----------------------     ------
    ADMIN SERVICES              D01
    WELD LINE AUTOMATION        D01
    WELD LINE PLANNING          B01

    3 record(s) selected.
```

The report shows that we have three projects that have the specified department numbers we used as parameter markers, two projects for department 'D01' and one for department 'B01'. This is another good example of how parameter markers can be very useful in your programs. You can store the needed data in a file or feed it as parameters to the Python program and change the report without any modifications to this Python script.

Producing Multiple Reports with Parameter Markers

The Listing 8-7 shows how to create multiple reports with a single SQL statement with parameter markers. As you will see, this is actually easier than it sounds.

Again, we will be using the basic code from the first example in this project to produce the report while only showing the modified code.

Listing 8-7. Producing Multiple Reports with One SQL Statement

.

.

.

```python
# get the records from the database
sqlstmt = """SELECT empno, firstnme, midinit, lastname, salary
 FROM employee WHERE salary < ? and salary > ?
 ORDER BY salary"""
prepstmt = ibm_db.prepare(connID, sqlstmt)
if prepstmt is False:
    print("Unable to prepare the statement.")
    exit(-1)
salaries = (('35000.00', '0.00'), ('50000.00', '40000.00'))
for i in (salaries):
    (salary1, salary2) = i
    retcode = ibm_db.bind_param(prepstmt, 1, salary1, ibm_db.SQL_PARAM_INPUT, \
                        ibm_db.SQL_CHAR)
    retcode = ibm_db.bind_param(prepstmt, 2, salary2, ibm_db.SQL_PARAM_INPUT, \
                        ibm_db.SQL_CHAR)
    results = ibm_db.execute(prepstmt)
    headerLines = getColNamesWidths(prepstmt)
    titleLines = populateColTitleLines(headerLines)
    dataLines = populateLines(prepstmt, headerLines)
    selrecords = len(dataLines)

    #print the result lines
    for line in titleLines:
        print(line)
    for line in dataLines:
        print(line)
    # print the number of records returned
    print('\n    ' + str(selrecords) + ' record(s) selected.\n')
```

.

.

.

At first glance, this listing looks a little different from our other examples. The main reason is that we have moved the report printing code into the loop. We do this because we need a report printed for each invocation of the `ibm_db.execute()` function.

Our SQL statement is slightly more complicated because we have added an ORDER BY clause at the end so that the output is ordered. It still has two parameter markers that specify a range of salaries.

Next, we prepare the SQL statement and test the outcome for errors.

The next statement sets up a Python array of lists that specify the range of salaries we want. There are two ranges specified, and each range will be used in separate invocations of the `ibm_db.execute()` function.

The rest of the code is a loop that takes a list of `salary` values to query the `employee` table. The code works just like the previous examples except that the report printing code has been moved inside the loop so that both queries are able to print their report.

One of the things to note in this example is that we did not have to prepare the SQL statement multiple times. This is by design so that the prepared SQL statement can be used multiple times just as our example does. Rebinding new values to the parameter markers and then executing the statement are all that needs to be done to produce possibly different reports.

Listing 8-8 provides the output from this example.

Listing 8-8. Multiple Reports from a Single SQL Statement

```
$ ../examples/example8-4.py
Enter the Db2 userid to be used: db2inst1
Password for db2inst1:
  EMPNO   FIRSTNME      MIDINIT  LASTNAME          SALARY
  ------  ------------  -------  ---------------   -----------

  200340  ROY           R        ALONZO               31840.00

     1 record(s) selected.


  EMPNO   FIRSTNME      MIDINIT  LASTNAME          SALARY
  ------  ------------  -------  ---------------   -----------

  000230  JAMES         J        JEFFERSON            42180.00
  000340  JASON         R        GOUNOT               43840.00
  000170  MASATOSHI     J        YOSHIMURA            44680.00
```

000330	WING		LEE	45370.00
200280	EILEEN	R	SCHWARTZ	46250.00
200010	DIAN	J	HEMMINGER	46500.00
000260	SYBIL	P	JOHNSON	47250.00
000240	SALVATORE	M	MARINO	48760.00
000250	DANIEL	S	SMITH	49180.00
000120	SEAN		O'CONNELL	49250.00
000220	JENNIFER	K	LUTZ	49840.00

```
11 record(s) selected.
```

We have successfully produced two reports on two different salary ranges and ordered the records by the salary field. The only change we made to the report printing code was to add a newline character at the end of the report so the two reports have some spacing between them.

Using Parameter Markers Without Binding Variables

This example is best used when you have a lot of data to load or update into a table. The ibm_db.execute() function has an additional optional parameter that can be used to pass parameter marker values instead of calling the ibm_db.bind_param() function for each parameter marker.

This use of ibm_db.execute() works best when the rows to be inserted/updated come from a file or another external resource. In our example, we use a file that contains rows to be inserted into the employee table. The file is constructed as a comma-separated values (CSV) file with each row of data representing a new row to be added to the employee table.

The added problem to be solved in this example is converting each row of data from the input file from a single string to a set of values for a Python tuple, which is what is required by the ibm_db.execute() function. We will go into this in more detail after the Listing 8-9 is shown.

Listing 8-9. Parameter Markers Without Binding Variables

```python
#!/usr/bin/python

import sys, getpass
import ibm_db

# main program
driver = "{IBM DB2 ODBC DRIVER}"   # Db2 driver information
host = '192.168.1.201'             # database host IP or dns address
port = "50000"                     # host port
db = "sample"                      # database registered name
uid = None                         # userid on the database host
pw = None                          # password of the uid
autocommit = ''                    # autocommit default override
connecttype = ''                   # connect type default override
uid = input("Enter the Db2 userid to be used: ")
pw = getpass.getpass(prompt = "Password for %s: " % uid)
if pw == None or pw == '':
    print("The password you entered is incorrect.")
    exit(-1)
conn_str = 'DRIVER=' + driver + ';HOSTNAME=' + host + \
           ';PORT=' + port + ';DATABASE=' + db + \
           ';UID=' + uid + ';PWD=' + pw
connID = ibm_db.connect(conn_str, autocommit, connecttype)
# If the connection fails for any reason an uncaught exception is thrown
# and the program will exit with an error.

# Add new designer employees to the employee table
sql = """INSERT INTO employee (empno, firstnme, midinit, lastname,
        workdept, phoneno, hiredate, job, edlevel, sex, birthdate,
        salary, bonus, comm) VALUES
        (?, ?, ?, ?, ?, ?, ?, ?, ?, ?, ?, ?, ?, ?)"""
stmt = ibm_db.prepare(connID, sql)
if stmt:
    inserts = 0
    with open('./example8-5.csv') as f:
```

```
        line = f.readline()
        while len(line) > 0:
            emp_list = line.split(',')
            for i in range(0, len(emp_list)):
                emp_list[i] = emp_list[i].rstrip("' \n")
                emp_list[i] = emp_list[i].lstrip("' ")
            emp = tuple(emp_list)
            result = ibm_db.execute(stmt, emp)
            if result is False:
                print("Unable to execute the SQL statement.")
                exit(-1)
            inserts += 1
            line = f.readline()
    print(str(inserts) + ' employees inserted successfully.')
# Now delete those new employees
ibm_db.exec_immediate(connID, "delete from employee where empno = '000350'")
ibm_db.exec_immediate(connID, "delete from employee where empno = '000360'")
ibm_db.exec_immediate(connID, "delete from employee where empno = '000370'")
ibm_db.exec_immediate(connID, "delete from employee where empno = '000380'")
print('4 employees deleted successfully.')

ibm_db.close(connID)
exit(0)
```

The first statements are the standard Python import statements needed for our program.

The next section of code is our standard setup for accessing a Db2 database, prompting the user for a userid and password, and connecting to the Db2 database.

The next section of code is different from our previous examples. We set up an SQL INSERT statement with parameter markers for each column of data we will insert. In this case, that happens to be all the columns in the employee table. Next, we prepare the statement for eventual execution.

The next block of code is where all the work happens. We open the file containing the information to be inserted into the table first. Then we read it in a line at a time. Next, since the file is a CSV construct, we split the line at each comma. The split pieces have data we do not need in each fragment, so we eliminate the leading and trailing spaces and the single quotes. Finally, we change the Python list of column values into a Python tuple.

Now we can call `ibm_db.execute()` with our `tuple` of column values as the second parameter in the function call. We then check to make sure that the `insert` works and then read in the next line.

The last thing we do is to delete the lines we added to the `employee` table. This will keep the database in its original state.

Last, we close the database connection.

Listing 8-10 shows all the output from the program. There is not much to see here, but this is what you should see as a result of the program executing successfully.

Listing 8-10. Output from Listing 8-9

```
$ ./example8-5.py
Enter the Db2 userid to be used: db2inst1
Password for db2inst1:
4 employees inserted successfully.
4 employees deleted successfully.
```

What this example shows is that you can eliminate 14 calls to the `ibm_db.bind_param()` function with a little work inside a loop. It also eliminates the use of 14 different variables to hold the information and replaces them with a simple Python `list` and a single `tuple`.

We should add another note here to possibly clear up an item. Tuples in Python are immutable. It means that once they are created, they cannot be modified or extended with additional members. That is why we had to convert the Python `list`, once it was ready, to a `tuple` in one call.

Joining Tables

Db2 supports the joining of tables in queries. There are two types of joins – inner and outer joins. Inner joins have been supported since the inception of Db2, but outer joins are a relatively new concept. We will discuss both types in this section.

Inner Joins

Inner joins have two forms in SQL. The first form of an inner join dates back to the beginning of Db2 and is rather straightforward to code. The second form of an inner join is just as easy to code and is much easier to determine exactly what is being joined and how it is being joined.

The following Listing 8-11 shows the old form of an inner join. This is only an excerpt of the entire program just to show the SQL statement and how it is processed.

Listing 8-11. The Old Form of an Inner Join

```
# get the records from the database
sqlstmt = """SELECT e.empno, e.lastname, d.deptname FROM emp e, dept d
    WHERE e.workdept = d.deptno AND d.deptname = ?"""
prepstmt = ibm_db.prepare(connID, sqlstmt)
if prepstmt is False:
    print("Unable to prepare the statement.")
    exit(-1)
deptnme = 'SOFTWARE SUPPORT'
retcode = ibm_db.bind_param(prepstmt, 1, deptnme, ibm_db.SQL_PARAM_INPUT, \
                            ibm_db.SQL_CHAR)
results = ibm_db.execute(prepstmt)
headerLines = getColNamesWidths(prepstmt)
titleLines = populateColTitleLines(headerLines)
dataLines = populateLines(prepstmt, headerLines)
selrecords = len(dataLines)
```

The output from this program will display only the employees working in the department known as "SOFTWARE SUPPORT." There should only be a total of six employees in that department. The two tables are joined in the workdept column in the employee table and the deptno column in the department table. An additional constraint asks only to see rows where the deptname is equal to "SOFTWARE SUPPORT."

As you can see, this example is pretty straightforward. Problems happen when the SQL statement has many constraints and the joined columns are not easily spotted in the SQL statement. To resolve this issue and to easily support outer joins, a new clause was added to the SQL statement that explicitly specifies the type of join.

The following Listing 8-12 shows the new syntax for an inner join, which obtains the same data as the previous example.

Listing 8-12. The New Form of an Inner Join

```
# get the records from the database
sqlstmt = """SELECT e.empno, e.lastname, d.deptname FROM emp e
    INNER JOIN dept d ON e.workdept = d.deptno AND d.deptname = ?"""
prepstmt = ibm_db.prepare(connID, sqlstmt)
if prepstmt is False:
    print("Unable to prepare the statement.")
    exit(-1)
deptnme = 'SOFTWARE SUPPORT'
retcode = ibm_db.bind_param(prepstmt, 1, deptnme, ibm_db.SQL_PARAM_INPUT, \
                        ibm_db.SQL_CHAR)
results = ibm_db.execute(prepstmt)
headerLines = getColNamesWidths(prepstmt)
titleLines = populateColTitleLines(headerLines)
dataLines = populateLines(prepstmt, headerLines)
selrecords = len(dataLines)
```

The only thing modified in this example is the SQL statement. Otherwise, the program is unchanged. The SQL statement has a new clause – the INNER JOIN clause and the subclause ON. These explicitly state that an inner join is being made on the two tables specified. There is no WHERE clause as the ON clause replaces it in this case.

The output from this program is exactly the same as the previous program. The reason both examples are shown here is that there are still a large number of programs still using the old form of an inner join and it is important to recognize and deal with these programs as needed.

Outer Joins

What makes an outer join different from an inner join is its ability to not only show you result rows similar to the inner join but also rows where the join columns from both tables are set to NULL. Thus, it displays rows that can never be joined together because one of the columns has an invalid value.

This is actually a rarely used feature of Db2, and thus we will not attempt to show an example here. For more information, refer to the IBM Db2 Knowledge Center on the Web.

Inserts, Updates, and Deletes

In this section, we will look at SQL insert, update, and delete statements and how they relate to Python and parameter markers. We actually saw delete statements in the previous section's example, but here we will discuss all these statements in more detail.

Listing 8-13 is an example of using all four SQL data manipulation statements. It inserts a new entry into the employee table, updates it, fetches it for display, and then deletes the entry. This will maintain the employee table in its original state.

Listing 8-13. Insert, Update, and Delete Example

```python
#!/usr/bin/python

import sys, getpass
from decimal import *
import ibm_db

# main program
driver = "{IBM DB2 ODBC DRIVER}"   # Db2 driver information
host = '192.168.1.201'             # database host IP or dns address
port = "50000"                     # host port
db = "sample"                      # database registered name
uid = None                         # userid on the database host
pw = None                          # password of the uid
autocommit = ''                    # autocommit default override
connecttype = ''                   # connect type default override
uid = input("Enter the Db2 userid to be used: ")
pw = getpass.getpass(prompt = "Password for %s: " % uid)
if pw == None or pw == '':
    print("The password you entered is incorrect.")
    exit(-1)
conn_str = 'DRIVER=' + driver + ';HOSTNAME=' + host + \
           ';PORT=' + port + ';DATABASE=' + db + \
           ';UID=' + uid + ';PWD=' + pw
connID = ibm_db.connect(conn_str, autocommit, connecttype)
# If the connection fails for any reason an uncaught exception is thrown
# and the program will exit with an error.
```

```
# Add new designer employees to the employee table
sql = """INSERT INTO employee (empno, firstnme, midinit, lastname,
         workdept, phoneno, hiredate, job, edlevel, sex, birthdate,
         salary, bonus, comm) VALUES
         (?, ?, ?, ?, ?, ?, ?, ?, ?, ?, ?, ?, ?, ?)"""
stmt = ibm_db.prepare(connID, sql)
if stmt is False:
    print("Unable to prepare the SQL statement.")
    exit(-1)
emp = ('000350', 'DAVID', 'W', 'ANDREWS', 'D11', '3634', '1969-03-20', \
    'DESIGNER', 20, 'M', '1951-06-14', 40160.00,  500, 2220)
result = ibm_db.execute(stmt, emp)
if result is False:
    print("Unable to execute the SQL statement.")
    ibm_db.close(connID)
    exit(-1)
# Now update the salary
sql = "UPDATE employee SET salary = ? where empno = '000350'"
stmt = ibm_db.prepare(connID, sql)
if stmt is False:
    print("Unable to prepare the SQL statement.")
    exit(-1)
salary = str(Decimal('40160.00') * Decimal('1.1'))
retcode = ibm_db.bind_param(stmt, 1, salary, ibm_db.SQL_PARAM_INPUT, \
                            ibm_db.SQL_CHAR)
result = ibm_db.execute(stmt)
if result is False:
    print("Unable to execute the SQL statement.")
    ibm_db.close(connID)
    exit(-1)
# Ensure the salary is updated
sql = "select empno, salary from employee where empno = '000350'"
results = ibm_db.exec_immediate(connID, sql)
if results is False:
    print("\nERROR: Unable to execute the SQL statement specified.")
```

```
    ibm_db.close(connID)
    exit(-1)
(empno, salary) = ibm_db.fetch_tuple(results)
print('empno: ', str(empno), '  old salary: 40160.00  new salary: ', str(salary))
# Now delete the employee we added
ibm_db.exec_immediate(connID, "delete from employee where empno =
'000350'")

ibm_db.close(connID)
exit(0)
```

The example listing starts out the same as all of our examples, with one exception. In order to update the salary, which internally is a decimal field, we need to import the decimal module. This way we can keep the adjustment consistent with the SQL field.

The first task is to insert a new record into the employee table. We use parameter fields in an INSERT statement. That is what all the question marks are in the SQL statement. We then call ibm_db.prepare() to prepare the statement.

Next, we create the tuple for the data to be inserted. Then, we call ibm_db.execute() to insert the new row into the database.

The next task is to update the record we just inserted. We create the SQL UPDATE statement with a single parameter marker for the new salary and then prepare the statement. The next statement converts the current salary to a decimal field as well as increases it by 10%. The result of this is a new field that is also a decimal field. We then bind the new salary to the UPDATE SQL statement and execute the statement.

Just to make sure the update succeeded and to prove to ourselves that it worked, we fetch the data from the database with a SELECT statement and display the results. The results display the employee number, the old salary, and the new salary.

Last, we delete the new row to get the database back to its original starting state.

This example is a little convoluted, but it is an example of all the SQL data manipulation statements. This example can also be used as a starting point for many of the types of activities you will encounter almost every day.

Listing 8-14 has the output from Listing 8-13. It shows the salary of the new employee both before and after the update.

Listing 8-14. Output from Listing 8-13

```
$ ./example8-6.py
Enter the Db2 userid to be used: db2inst1
Password for db2inst1:
empno:  000350   old salary: 40160.00  new salary:  44176.00
```

It is important to note that the calculation of the 10% increase is exactly correct and does not suffer from the inaccuracies from a floating-point calculation. By using the `decimal` package to perform the calculation, we have ensured the correct increase was applied.

Some Other ibm_db APIs

In this section, we will look at some other `ibm_db` package APIs that you may have occasion to use. These are not data manipulation statements, but instead can provide information about various aspects of the database and the processing environment of your Python program.

It should be noted that this does not cover all the remaining APIs in the `ibm_db` package. The remaining APIs are rarely used and are sufficiently documented so they can be easily incorporated in your programs.

Listing 8-15 shows the code for this example. We will examine it after the listing.

Listing 8-15. Some Miscellaneous ibm_db APIs

```
#!/usr/bin/python

import sys, getpass
import ibm_db

# main program
driver = "{IBM DB2 ODBC DRIVER}"  # Db2 driver information
host = '192.168.1.201'            # database host IP or dns address
port = "50000"                    # host port
db = "sample"                     # database registered name
uid = None                        # userid on the database host
pw = None                         # password of the uid
autocommit = ''                   # autocommit default override
connecttype = ''                  # connect type default override
```

```python
uid = input("Enter the Db2 userid to be used: ")
pw = getpass.getpass(prompt = "Password for %s: " % uid)
if pw == None or pw == '':
    print("The password you entered is incorrect.")
    exit(-1)
conn_str = 'DRIVER=' + driver + ';HOSTNAME=' + host + \
           ';PORT=' + port + ';DATABASE=' + db + \
           ';UID=' + uid + ';PWD=' + pw
connID = ibm_db.connect(conn_str, autocommit, connecttype)
# If the connection fails for any reason an uncaught exception is thrown
# and the program will exit with an error.

# Test if the connection is active
active = ibm_db.active(connID)
if active:
    print('The currect connection is active.')
else:
    print('*The current connection is not active.')
# Test autocommit
commit = ibm_db.autocommit(connID)
if active:
    print('Autocommit is active.')
else:
    print('*Autocommit is not active.')
# Get the client info
clientinfo = ibm_db.client_info(connID)
if clientinfo:
    print('Client info:')
    print('  APPL_CODEPAGE: ', clientinfo.APPL_CODEPAGE)
    print('  CONN_CODEPAGE: ', clientinfo.CONN_CODEPAGE)
    print('  DATA_SOURCE_NAME: ', clientinfo.DATA_SOURCE_NAME)
    print('  DRIVER_NAME: ', clientinfo.DRIVER_NAME)
    print('  DRIVER_ODBC_VER: ', clientinfo.DRIVER_ODBC_VER)
    print('  DRIVER_VER: ', clientinfo.DRIVER_VER)
    print('  ODBC_SQL_CONFORMANCE: ', clientinfo.ODBC_SQL_CONFORMANCE)
    print('  ODBC_VER: ', clientinfo.ODBC_VER)
```

```
else:
    print('Could not obtain client info.')
# Get column priviliges, if they exist
priv = ibm_db.column_privileges(connID, None, uid.upper(), 'employee', 'workdept')
row = ibm_db.fetch_assoc(priv)
if row:
    print('Sample database, table department, column priviliges:')
    print("   Schema name            : {}" .format(row['TABLE_SCHEM']))
    print("   Table name             : {}" .format(row['TABLE_NAME']))
    print("   Column name            : {}" .format(row['COLUMN_NAME']))
    print("   Privilege grantor      : {}" .format(row['GRANTOR']))
    print("   Privilege recipient    : {}" .format(row['GRANTEE']))
    print("   Privilege              : {}" .format(row['PRIVILEGE']))
    print("   Privilege is grantable : {}" .format(row['IS_GRANTABLE']))
else:
    print('No column privileges to retrieve.')
# Get column metadata, if it exists
coldata = ibm_db.columns(connID, None, None, 'employee', 'empno')
row = ibm_db.fetch_assoc(coldata)
if row:
    print('Sample database, table department, columns metadata:')
    table_name = row['TABLE_NAME']
    column_name = row['COLUMN_NAME']
    print("   Table name   : {}" .format(table_name))
    print("     Column name : {}" .format(column_name))
else:
    print('No column metadata to retrieve.')
# Test SQL commit
rc = ibm_db.commit(connID)
if rc:
    print('Commit succeeded.')
else:
    print('*Commit did not succeed.')

ibm_db.close(connID)
exit(0)
```

As always, the program has the same starting code as our other examples. The first test is the `ibm_db.active()` API. This API determines if the connection passed as a parameter is still active. While not usually important in most programs, it is used in programs that use the `ibm_db.pconnect()` API.

The next API used is the `ibm_db.autocommit()`. This API can both get and set the AUTOCOMMIT flag for the specified connection.

The next API is the `ibm_db.client_info()`. This API returns information about the client side of the connection. It lists the code pages used, the driver names and versions, and the SQL standard conformance.

Next, the `ibm_db.column_priviliges()` queries tables about the privileges assigned to specific columns. These privileges may or may not exist. The tables in the sample database usually do not have special privileges assigned to them, so the API does not return any data from them.

The `ibm_db.columns()` API is used to query the metadata that has been assigned to a column in a table. The sample database has no metadata assigned to columns that we have been able to determine.

The last API we test is the `ibm_db.commit()` API. This API forces a COMMIT to the database at the point it is called. This should work whether the AUTOCOMMIT flag is on or not.

Listing 8-16 shows the output of Listing 8-15 on an example client machine.

Listing 8-16. Output from the Listing 8-15 Program

```
$ ./example8-7.py
Enter the Db2 userid to be used: db2inst1
Password for db2inst1:
The currect connection is active.
Autocommit is active.
Client info:
  APPL_CODEPAGE:  1208
  CONN_CODEPAGE:  1208
  DATA_SOURCE_NAME:  SAMPLE
  DRIVER_NAME:  libdb2.a
  DRIVER_ODBC_VER:  03.51
  DRIVER_VER:  11.01.0405
  ODBC_SQL_CONFORMANCE:  EXTENDED
```

```
  ODBC_VER:   03.01.0000
No column privileges to retrieve.
No column metadata to retrieve.
Commit succeeded.
```

This output from is pretty simple. Mostly, just one line results from the API being tested. The client info API has more data, all of it of interest to the programmer who requires the information.

Creating Database Objects

The ibm_db library can also help you create database objects such as tables, indexes, and tablespaces. It can also remove existing database objects when necessary. These actions are done through the CREATE and DROP SQL statements.

In addition, this section will cover two more ibm_db APIs, the stmt_error and the stmt_errormsg. These APIs are used to report error conditions and explanations. They can be used after the prepare(), exec_immediate(), and callproc() APIs and contain information that will help you to diagnose the problem with your SQL statement.

Listing 8-17 shows how to create a table using the Python module. A word of note: The example that follows has no real meaning but is used strictly for showing examples of table column definitions.

Listing 8-17. Creating a Sample Table

```
#!/usr/bin/python

import sys, getpass
import ibm_db

# main program
driver = "{IBM DB2 ODBC DRIVER}"   # Db2 driver information
host = '192.168.1.201'             # database host IP or dns address
port = "50000"                     # host port
db = "sample"                      # database registered name
uid = None                         # userid on the database host
pw = None                          # password of the uid
autocommit = ''                    # autocommit default override
connecttype = ''                   # connect type default override
```

```python
uid = input("Enter the Db2 userid to be used: ")
pw = getpass.getpass(prompt = "Password for %s: " % uid)
if pw == None or pw == '':
    print("The password you entered is incorrect.")
    exit(-1)
conn_str = 'DRIVER=' + driver + ';HOSTNAME=' + host + \
           ';PORT=' + port + ';DATABASE=' + db + \
           ';UID=' + uid + ';PWD=' + pw
connID = ibm_db.connect(conn_str, autocommit, connecttype)
# If the connection fails for any reason an uncaught exception is thrown
# and the program will exit with an error.

# create the sample table
sqlstmt = """CREATE TABLE myexampletable (
    C01         INTEGER NOT NULL
                GENERATED ALWAYS AS IDENTITY
                (START WITH 1, INCREMENT BY 1),
    C02         CHAR(50),
    C03         VARCHAR(70),
    C04         DEC(15,2),
    C05         FLOAT(21),
    C06         CLOB(1K),
    C07         VARGRAPHIC(2000),
    C08         BLOB(1M),
    C09         DATE,
    C10         TIME,
    C11         TIMESTAMP,
    C12         XML,
    C13         BOOLEAN,
    PRIMARY KEY(C01))"""
try:
    rc = ibm_db.exec_immediate(connID, sqlstmt)
except:
    print("Create ' {} ' failed with ".format(sqlstmt))
    print("Error : {}".format(ibm_db.stmt_errormsg()))
    exit(-1)
```

```
print('\n    The CREATE statement executed successfully.')
```

```
ibm_db.close(connID)
exit(0)
```

There are a few things to note about this example. First, the table is meaningless except as an example. It is not tied to any other table in the sample database. It is just an example of some of the column data types available to the user by Db2.

Second, the try/except block adds some nice exception processing. It looks for a non-zero return code from the exec_immidiate() API, and if not found it executes the except block of code.

Third, the except block has a call to the stmt_errormsg() API, which will print out the error message associated with the error in the SQL statement.

Fourth, there is no formatting code in this example because it does not return a result table, just a simple return code.

The C01 column is an example of an incrementing column. Each time a new row is inserted or altered, the database will generate a value to be placed in this column. This column is also the primary key for the table as defined by the last clause in the SQL statement.

The C02 is a character string that always has 50 characters associated with it. When you assign a character string to this column that is shorter than 50 characters, the system will pad the string on the right with blanks until it is 50 characters long. If you try to add a string longer than 50 characters, it will be truncated to 50 characters.

The C03 column is a variable character string. This type of string is not padded on the right with blanks. Instead, the actual length of the string is recorded. But if the string is longer than 70 characters, it will be truncated to 70 characters.

The C04 column is a fixed decimal number with a length of 15 numeric values with 2 decimal places.

The C05 column is a floating-point field that can hold a total of 21 numeric characters.

The C06 column is a variable graphic field with a maximum of 1,000,000 bytes.

The C07 column is a variable graphic field with a maximum of 200 bytes.

The C08 column is a binary LOB with a length of 1,000,000 bytes.

The C09 column is a field that contains a data value.

The C10 column is a field that contains a time value.

The C11 column is a field that contains a timestamp value. This field contains both a date and a time value concatenated together to form an instance of time and date.

The C12 column is an XML field. This field actually is a pointer to the file system that contains the XML data.

The C13 column is a Boolean field for simple yes/no values.

Now that we have looked at this table, you may want to remove it from the database. Listing 8-18 will do that for you.

Listing 8-18. Removing a Table

```python
#!/usr/bin/python

import sys, getpass
import ibm_db

# main program
driver = "{IBM DB2 ODBC DRIVER}"  # Db2 driver information
host = '192.168.1.201'            # database host IP or dns address
port = "50000"                    # host port
db = "sample"                     # database registered name
uid = None                        # userid on the database host
pw = None                         # password of the uid
autocommit = ''                   # autocommit default override
connecttype = ''                  # connect type default override
uid = input("Enter the Db2 userid to be used: ")
pw = getpass.getpass(prompt = "Password for %s: " % uid)
if pw == None or pw == '':
    print("The password you entered is incorrect.")
    exit(-1)
conn_str = 'DRIVER=' + driver + ';HOSTNAME=' + host + \
        ';PORT=' + port + ';DATABASE=' + db + \
            ';UID=' + uid + ';PWD=' + pw
connID = ibm_db.connect(conn_str, autocommit, connecttype)
# If the connection fails for any reason an uncaught exception is thrown
# and the program will exit with an error.

# create the sample table
sqlstmt = """DROP TABLE myexampletable"""
```

```
try:
    rc = ibm_db.exec_immediate(connID, sqlstmt)
except:
    print("Drop ' {} ' failed with ".format(sqlstmt))
    print("Error : {}".format(ibm_db.stmt_errormsg()))
    exit(-1)
print('\n    The DROP statement executed successfully.')

ibm_db.close(connID)
exit(0)
```

This program is very similar to the previous one except that it uses the DROP SQL statement to remove the table we created at the beginning of this section.

Obtaining Attributes of an Existing Table

Sometimes you may need to know the attributes of each column in an existing Db2 table. With the ibm_db library, you can easily obtain these attributes. Listing 8-19 shows how to accomplish this.

Listing 8-19. Obtaining the Column Attributes of an Existing Table

```
#!/usr/bin/python

import sys, getpass
import ibm_db

# main program
resultSet = False
dataRecord = False
tableName = "EMP"
sqlDataTypes = {0 : "SQL_UNKNOWN_TYPE", 1 : "SQL_CHAR", 2 : "SQL_NUMERIC",
3 : "SQL_DECIMAL",
    4 : "SQL_INTEGER", 5 : "SQL_SMALLINT", 6 : "SQL_FLOAT", 7 : "SQL_REAL",
    8 : "SQL_DOUBLE",
    9 : "SQL_DATETIME", 12 : "SQL_VARCHAR", 16 : "SQL_BOOLEAN", 19 : "SQL_ROW",
    91 : "SQL_TYPE_DATE", 92 : "SQL_TYPE_TIME", 93 : "SQL_TYPE_TIMESTAMP",
```

```
  95 : "SQL_TYPE_TIMESTAMP_WITH_TIMEZONE", -8 : "SQL_WCHAR",
  -9 : "SQL_WVARCHAR",
 -10 : "SQL_WLONGVARCHAR", -95 : "SQL_GRAPHIC", -96 : "SQL_VARGRAPHIC",
 -97 : "SQL_LONGVARGRAPHIC", -98 : "SQL_BLOB", -99 : "SQL_CLOB",
 -350 : "SQL_DBCLOB",
 -360 : "SQL_DECFLOAT", -370 : "SQL_XML", -380 : "SQL_CURSORHANDLE",
 -400 : "SQL_DATALINK",
 -450 : "SQL_USER_DEFINED_TYPE"}
sqlDateTimeSubtypes = {1 : "SQL_CODE_DATE", 2 : "SQL_CODE_TIME", 3 : "SQL_
CODE_TIMESTAMP",
    4 : "SQL_CODE_TIMESTAMP_WITH_TIMEZONE"}
driver = "{IBM DB2 ODBC DRIVER}"  # Db2 driver information
host = '192.168.1.201'            # database host IP or dns address
port = "50000"                    # host port
db = "sample"                     # database registered name
uid = None                        # userid on the database host
pw = None                         # password of the uid
autocommit = ''                   # autocommit default override
connecttype = ''                  # connect type default override
uid = input("Enter the Db2 userid to be used: ")
pw = getpass.getpass(prompt = "Password for %s: " % uid)
if pw == None or pw == '':
    print("The password you entered is incorrect.")
    exit(-1)
conn_str = 'DRIVER=' + driver + ';HOSTNAME=' + host + \
           ';PORT=' + port + ';DATABASE=' + db + \
           ';UID=' + uid + ';PWD=' + pw
connID = ibm_db.connect(conn_str, '', '')
# If the connection fails for any reason an uncaught exception is thrown
# and the program will exit with an error.

# Attempt to retrieve information about all columns of a table
resultSet = ibm_db.columns(connID, None, None, tableName, None)
# If The Information Desired Could Not Be Retrieved, Display An Error
  Message And Exit
if resultSet is False:
```

```python
        print("\nERROR: Unable to obtain the information desired\n.")
        conn.closeConnection()
        exit(-1)
noData = False
loopCounter = 1
while noData is False:
    dataRecord = ibm_db.fetch_assoc(resultSet)
    if dataRecord is False:
        noData = True
    else:
        # Display Record Header Information
        print("Column " + str(loopCounter) + " details:")
        print("_____")
        # Display The Information Stored In The Data Record Retrieved
        print("Table schema             : {}" .format(dataRecord['TABLE_SCHEM']))
        print("Table name               : {}" .format(dataRecord['TABLE_NAME']))
        print("Column name              : {}" .format(dataRecord['COLUMN_NAME']))
        print("Data type                : {}" .format(dataRecord['TYPE_NAME']))
        print("Size                     : {}" .format(dataRecord['COLUMN_SIZE']))
        print("Buffer size              : {}" .format(dataRecord['BUFFER_LENGTH']))
        print("Scale (decimal digits)   : ", end="")
        if dataRecord['DECIMAL_DIGITS'] == None:
            print("Not applicable")
        else:
            print("{}" .format(dataRecord['DECIMAL_DIGITS']))
        print("Precision radix          : ", end="")
        if dataRecord['NUM_PREC_RADIX'] == 10:
            print("Exact numeric data type")
        elif dataRecord['NUM_PREC_RADIX'] == 2:
            print("Approximate numeric data type")
        elif dataRecord['NUM_PREC_RADIX'] == None:
            print("Not applicable")
        print("Can accept NULL values   : ", end="")
        if dataRecord['NULLABLE'] == ibm_db.SQL_FALSE:
```

```
        print("NO")
    elif dataRecord['NULLABLE'] == ibm_db.SQL_TRUE:
        print("YES")
    print("Remarks                    : {}" .format(dataRecord['REMARKS']))
    print("Default value              : {}" .format(dataRecord['COLUMN_DEF']))
    print("SQL data type              : ", end="")
    print(sqlDataTypes.get(dataRecord['SQL_DATA_TYPE']))
    print("SQL data/time subtype    : ", end="")
    print(sqlDateTimeSubtypes.get(dataRecord['SQL_DATETIME_SUB']))
    print("Data type                  : {}" .format(dataRecord['DATA_
    TYPE']))
    print("Length in octets           : ", end="")
    if dataRecord['CHAR_OCTET_LENGTH'] == None:
        print("Not applicable")
    else:
        print("{}" .format(dataRecord['CHAR_OCTET_LENGTH']))
    print("Ordinal position            : {}" .format(dataRecord['ORDINAL_
                                        POSITION']))
    print("Can contain NULL values  : {}" .format(dataRecord['IS_
                                        NULLABLE']))

    # Increment The loopCounter Variable And Print A Blank Line To
      Separate The
    # Records From Each Other
    loopCounter += 1
    print()

ibm_db.close(connID)
exit(0)
```

There are a number of attributes available for a column. Some of these will not be applicable depending on the data type defined on the column or through not being defined. The main attribute you will be interested in is the DATA TYPE or the SQL DATA TYPE, which determines the kind of data stored in the column. There are specific attributes that only apply to certain types of data, that is, the SCALE attribute for instance only applies to the DECIMAL data type.

Listing 8-20 lists all the columns in a table. In the following output, we have eliminated some of the columns in order to save space.

Listing 8-20. Output of Listing 8-19

```
$  ./example8-14.py
Enter the Db2 userid to be used: db2inst1
Password for db2inst1:
Column 1 details:

_____

Table schema              : DB2INST1
Table name                : EMP
Column name               : EMPNO
Data type                 : CHAR
Size                      : 6
Buffer size               : 6
Scale (decimal digits)    : Not applicable
Precision radix           : Not applicable
Can accept NULL values    : NO
Remarks                   : None
Default value             : None
SQL data type             : SQL_CHAR
SQL data/time subtype     : None
Data type                 : 1
Length in octets          : 6
Ordinal position          : 1
Can contain NULL values   : NO

Column 2 details:

_____

Table schema              : DB2INST1
Table name                : EMP
Column name               : FIRSTNME
Data type                 : VARCHAR
Size                      : 12
Buffer size               : 12
Scale (decimal digits)    : Not applicable
```

```
Precision radix        : Not applicable
Can accept NULL values : NO
Remarks                : None
Default value          : None
SQL data type          : SQL_VARCHAR
SQL data/time subtype  : None
Data type              : 12
Length in octets       : 12
Ordinal position       : 2
Can contain NULL values : NO
```

.

.

.

Column 14 details:

```
Table schema           : DB2INST1
Table name             : EMP
Column name            : COMM
Data type              : DECIMAL
Size                   : 9
Buffer size            : 11
Scale (decimal digits) : 2
Precision radix        : Exact numeric data type
Can accept NULL values : YES
Remarks                : None
Default value          : None
SQL data type          : SQL_DECIMAL
SQL data/time subtype  : None
Data type              : 3
Length in octets       : Not applicable
Ordinal position       : 14
Can contain NULL values : YES
```

Each column along with all attributes is shown in the complete output file. Listing 8-20 is just a small excerpt of the complete listing.

The Listing 8-14 Python program is very useful in a number of circumstances such as discovering if NULLs are allowed in a column, if there is a DEFAULT VALUE specified for a column, the SIZE attribute that can provide a clue as to the maximum size of a column, and many other attributes.

Obtaining Attributes of a Result Set

Unlike obtaining the attributes of an existing Db2 table, a result set is a temporary table that holds the result of a query. The reason we have this API is that a result set may be a joining of two or more tables and some columns may be modified in the join in such a way that their attributes are modified by the join process. Thus, it may be hard to determine the actual attributes on a joined column except thru trial and error.

Listing 8-21 demonstrates how to discover the attributes for a result set so that they can be used to help you determine how a column should be displayed.

Listing 8-21. Obtaining the Attributes of a Result Set

```python
#!/usr/bin/python

import sys, getpass
import ibm_db

# main program
resultSet = False
dataRecord = False
tableName = "EMP"
sqlDataTypes = {0 : "SQL_UNKNOWN_TYPE", 1 : "SQL_CHAR", 2 : "SQL_NUMERIC",
3 : "SQL_DECIMAL",
    4 : "SQL_INTEGER", 5 : "SQL_SMALLINT", 6 : "SQL_FLOAT", 7 : "SQL_REAL",
    8 : "SQL_DOUBLE",
    9 : "SQL_DATETIME", 12 : "SQL_VARCHAR", 16 : "SQL_BOOLEAN", 19 : "SQL_ROW",
   91 : "SQL_TYPE_DATE", 92 : "SQL_TYPE_TIME", 93 : "SQL_TYPE_TIMESTAMP",
   95 : "SQL_TYPE_TIMESTAMP_WITH_TIMEZONE", -8 : "SQL_WCHAR", -9 : "SQL_
        WVARCHAR",
  -10 : "SQL_WLONGVARCHAR", -95 : "SQL_GRAPHIC", -96 : "SQL_VARGRAPHIC",
  -97 : "SQL_LONGVARGRAPHIC", -98 : "SQL_BLOB", -99 : "SQL_CLOB",
  -350 : "SQL_DBCLOB",
```

```
  -360 : "SQL_DECFLOAT", -370 : "SQL_XML", -380 : "SQL_CURSORHANDLE",
  -400 : "SQL_DATALINK",
  -450 : "SQL_USER_DEFINED_TYPE"}
sqlDateTimeSubtypes = {1 : "SQL_CODE_DATE", 2 : "SQL_CODE_TIME", 3 : "SQL_
CODE_TIMESTAMP",
    4 : "SQL_CODE_TIMESTAMP_WITH_TIMEZONE"}
driver = "{IBM DB2 ODBC DRIVER}"  # Db2 driver information
host = '192.168.1.201'            # database host IP or dns address
port = "50000"                    # host port
db = "sample"                     # database registered name
uid = None                        # userid on the database host
pw = None                         # password of the uid
autocommit = ''                   # autocommit default override
connecttype = ''                  # connect type default override
uid = input("Enter the Db2 userid to be used: ")
pw = getpass.getpass(prompt = "Password for %s: " % uid)
if pw == None or pw == '':
    print("The password you entered is incorrect.")
    exit(-1)
conn_str = 'DRIVER=' + driver + ';HOSTNAME=' + host + \
           ';PORT=' + port + ';DATABASE=' + db + \
           ';UID=' + uid + ';PWD=' + pw
connID = ibm_db.connect(conn_str, '', '')
# If the connection fails for any reason an uncaught exception is thrown
# and the program will exit with an error.

# Attempt to retrieve information about all columns of a table
sqlstmt = """SELECT e.empno, e.lastname, d.deptname FROM emp e, dept d
    WHERE e.workdept = d.deptno AND d.deptname = ?"""
prepstmt = ibm_db.prepare(connID, sqlstmt)
if prepstmt is False:
    print("Unable to prepare the statement.")
    exit(-1)
deptnme = 'SOFTWARE SUPPORT'
```

```
retcode = ibm_db.bind_param(prepstmt, 1, deptnme, ibm_db.SQL_PARAM_INPUT, \
                            ibm_db.SQL_CHAR)
results = ibm_db.execute(prepstmt)
# If The Information Desired Could Not Be Retrieved, Display An Error
Message And Exit
if results is False:
    print("\nERROR: Unable to obtain the information desired\n.")
    ibm_db.close(connID)
    exit(-1)
loopCounter = 1
cols = ibm_db.num_fields(prepstmt)
while loopCounter <= cols:
    # Display Record Header Information
    print("Column " + str(loopCounter) + " details:")
    print("_____")
    # Display The Information Stored In The Data Record Retrieved
    print("Column name               : {}" .format(ibm_db.field_
                                        name(prepstmt, loopCounter)))
    print("Data type                 : {}" .format(ibm_db.field_
                                        type(prepstmt, loopCounter)))
    print("Size                      : {}" .format(ibm_db.field_display_
                                        size(prepstmt, loopCounter)))
    print("Scale (decimal digits)    : ", end="")
    if ibm_db.field_scale(prepstmt, loopCounter) == None:
        print("Not applicable")
    else:
        print("{}" .format(ibm_db.field_scale(prepstmt, loopCounter)))
    print("Precision                 : {}" .format(ibm_db.field_
                                        precision(prepstmt, loopCounter)))
    print("Display size              : ", end="")
    if ibm_db.field_display_size(prepstmt,loopCounter) == None:
        print("Not applicable")
    else:
        print("{}" .format(ibm_db.field_display_size(prepstmt,loopCounter)))

    # Increment The loopCounter Variable And Print A Blank Line To Separate The
```

```
    # Records From Each Other
    loopCounter += 1
    print()

ibm_db.close(connID)
exit(0)
```

This example is somewhat similar to the Listing 8-19 program except that there are fewer attributes available. This is mostly due to the nature of a result set, which is mostly for display purposes in a Python program.

Listing 8-22 is the output from the Listing 8-21 program.

Listing 8-22. Output from Listing 8-21

```
$ ./example8-15.py
Enter the Db2 userid to be used: db2inst1
Password for db2inst1:
Column 1 details:

Column name               : LASTNAME
Data type                 : string
Size                      : 15
Scale (decimal digits)    : 0
Precision                 : 15
Display size              : 15

Column 2 details:

Column name               : DEPTNAME
Data type                 : string
Size                      : 36
Scale (decimal digits)    : 0
Precision                 : 36
Display size              : 36
```

Column 3 details:

Column name	: False
Data type	: False
Size	: False
Scale (decimal digits)	: False
Precision	: False
Display size	: False

The output here is similar to Listing 8-14. The addition of the DISPLAY SIZE attribute is extremely valuable as this is the number of characters needed to properly display the column data.

ibm_db_dbi and Python

The ibm_db_dbi module is actually a Python script, but it can be imported just like a Python module. The module follows the PEP 249 Python Database API Specification v2.0, and this makes your programs portable across different databases – at least that is the general idea. The specification for this module is somewhat loose, and thus it leaves a lot of room for additions, which may not be portable to other databases. This is the case for ibm_db_dbi.

Listing 8-23 is an example of a Python program that uses the ibm_db_dbi module.

Listing 8-23. An ibm_db_dbi Example Python Program

```python
#!/usr/bin/python

import sys, getpass
import ibm_db_dbi

# main program
driver = "{IBM DB2 ODBC DRIVER}"   # Db2 driver information
host = '192.168.1.201'             # database host IP or dns address
port = "50000"                     # host port
db = "sample"                      # database registered name
uid = None                         # userid on the database host
```

```python
pw = None                               # password of the uid
autocommit = ''                         # autocommit default override
connecttype = ''                        # connect type default override
uid = input("Enter the Db2 userid to be used: ")
pw = getpass.getpass(prompt = "Password for %s: " % uid)
if pw == None or pw == '':
    print("The password you entered is incorrect.")
    exit(-1)
#host = host + ':' + port
conn_str = 'DRIVER=' + driver + ';HOSTNAME=' + host + \
           ';PORT=' + port + ';DATABASE=' + db + \
           ';UID=' + uid + ';PWD=' + pw
connID = ibm_db_dbi.connect(dsn=conn_str, conn_options=None)
# If the connection fails for any reason an uncaught exception is thrown
# and the program will exit with an error.

# get a cursor
cursor = connID.cursor()

sqlstmt = 'select * from department'
cursor.execute(sqlstmt)
# build/print header lines and fetch/print all rows
row = cursor.fetchone()
if row:
    rows = 0
    cols = len(cursor.description)
    col = 0
    typecode = []
    collen = []
    tline1 = ''
    tline2 = ''
    i = 0
    # print the report header lines
    while i < cols:
        (name,type_code,display_size,internal_size,precision,scale,null_ok) = \
          cursor.description[i]
```

```
        typecode.append(type_code)
        collen.append(max(display_size, len(name)))
        tline1 = tline1 + '  ' + name +  (collen[i]-len(name))*' '
        tline2 = tline2 + '  ' + (collen[i]*'-')
        i += 1
    print(tline1 + '\n' + tline2)
    # print each fetched row
    while row:
        rows += 1
        colvals = list(row)
        i = 0
        line = ''
        while i < cols:
            (name,type_code,display_size,internal_
            size,precision,scale,null_ok) = \
             cursor.description[i]
            if colvals[i] is None:
                line = line + '  -' + (collen[i]-1)*' '
            elif typecode[i] in ibm_db_dbi.DECIMAL:
                line = line + '  ' + (collen[i]-len(colvals[i]))*' ' + colvals[i]
            else:
                line = line + '  ' + colvals[i] + (collen[i]-len(colvals[i]))*' '
            i += 1
        print(line)
        row = cursor.fetchone()
    # print summary
    print('\n   ' + str(rows) + ' record(s) selected.')
connID.close()
exit(0)
```

The code in this example is pretty easy to follow. What is really noticeable is the reduced amount of Python code that was needed to produce the same output as Figure 1-1. This is somewhat misleading as the ibm_db_dbi module, which is also Python code, is doing a lot of the work we did for ourselves in Listing 8-1. Thus, about the same amount of Python code is being executed when the module and our program code are taken together.

Listing 8-24 shows that you can still use parameter markers in our SQL statements.

Listing 8-24. Using Parameter Markers with ibm_db_dbi

```
# get a cursor
cursor = connID.cursor()

sqlstmt = 'SELECT projname, deptno FROM project WHERE deptno = ? OR deptno = ?'
cursor.execute(sqlstmt, ('B01', 'D01'))
# build/print header lines and fetch/print all rows
```

We are just showing the changed statements needed in Listing 8-9 that utilize parameter markers. This changes the program to match the output of Listing 8-3. Note that the parameters are passed on the execute function as a tuple.

Once again, most of the code is the same as in the previous example. This again shows that using the ibm_db_dbi module, we can leverage it to reduce the code in our Python programs. Just be aware that you should try as hard as possible to not use code that cannot be ported.

Where Is the ibm_db Module Going?

In this chapter we have covered the ibm_db module in depth, but where is it going? A careful analysis of the module source code reveals that there are some incompatibilities with the Db2 APIs. The developers acknowledge that these problems should be fixed and are in the process of figuring out what to do. They also acknowledge the documentation for the module is lacking enough examples for many Python developers.

These and other module problems will certainly be fixed in future versions, but currently they do not pose too many problems. The module is certainly usable as is as we have shown in this book. But what can be done to improve things so that Db2 has an increased user base on Windows, Linux, and Unix? Currently, the IBM developers are creating Python modules that allow programs that use a generic database API to use Db2 as the main database by creating an interface from the program's generic interface to the ibm_db module. This will allow Db2 to store the objects needed by the program.

So far, the developers have developed four such interfaces, which we will discuss in the following.

The ibm_db_dbi Module

The ibm_db_dbi interface has been discussed in the previous section, but it is worth mentioning here. This interface is included when you install the ibm_db module. It is based on the PEP 248 specification. PEP 249 describes a generic interface that should support almost any native database query interface. The ibm_db_dbi interface fully supports this specification.

The previous section has an example of how to use the ibm_db_dbi interface. This interface calls APIs in the ibm_db interface to gain access to a Db2 database. But it is important to note that if your database changes in the future, the only change needed by your Python program is to modify the import statement so that it points to the interface file used by the new database.

By using a common generic database interface, your program becomes more portable and also much easier to maintain. The disadvantage to using a common database interface is that some of the more advanced features of a native database interface are lost to the programmer. So weigh these choices carefully when choosing your program's interface to a database.

The Django Database Interface

The Django system is a very powerful mechanism for building web-based pages. It has many useful features and is used by a large percentage of the web programmers around the world. Django also has a generic database interface that a database supplier can use to produce a translation to the API the database supports. This is very similar to the way the PEP 248 interface works. Db2 supplies the ibm_db_django module that performs the translations necessary to access Db2 from Django.

To install the ibm_db_django module, perform the following command:

```
sudo pip install ibm_db
sudo pip install ibm_db_django
```

This will install the latest version of the ibm_db_django and the ibm_db module on your machine. All that is left to do is configure the module in the Django configuration file, and you are ready to use Db2 as your storage facility for your Django application. Listing 8-25 shows what needs to be added to the Django settings.py file.

Listing 8-25. Django settings.py File Extract

```
DATABASES = {
    'default': {
        'ENGINE'    : 'ibm_db_django',
        'NAME'      : 'mydjangodb',
        'USER'      : 'db2inst1',
        'PASSWORD'  : 'xxxxxx2',
        'HOST'      : 'localhost',
        'PORT'      : '50000',
        'PCONNECT'  : True,      #Optional property, default is false
    }
}
```

The following lines will also need to be added to the tuple INSTALLED_APPS in the settings.py file.

```
'django.contrib.flatpages',
'django.contrib.redirects',
'django.contrib.comments',
'django.contrib.admin',
```

The generic Django database API is fully supported by the ibm_db_django module, so no special coding is needed in your Python application. However, you may need a Db2 administrator to establish the database on the Db2 server if you do not have permission to do so.

Django by default executes without transactions, that is, in auto-commit mode. This default is generally not what you want in web applications. You should remember to turn on transaction support in Django.

To learn more about Django, you should visit the www.djangoproject.com/ website.

The SQLAlchemy Adapter

SQLAlchemy is an object-relational adapter. It transforms object information in a Python program and maps it to a relational database to allow an object to be saved from one execution of the program to the next. The transform is performed via a set of well-known patterns so that reliability of the stored object is persistent.

The SQLAlchemy toolkit enjoys wide use in the Python universe because it uses well-established rules in the transform process. These tools are well understood and have a long history of use in other object-oriented languages as well.

To install the ibm_db_sa module, perform the following command:

```
sudo pip install ibm_db
sudo pip install ibm_db_sa
```

This will install the latest version of the ibm_db_sa and ibm_db module on your machine. All that is left to do is configure the module in the CLI configuration file, and you are ready to use Db2 as your storage facility for your SQLAlchemy application. Listing 8-26 shows what needs to be added to the CLI configuration file.

Listing 8-26. CLI Configuration File Extract

```
[pydb]
Database=pydev
Protocol=tcpip
Hostname=host.name.com
Servicename=50000
uid=db2inst1
pwd=secret
```

Once the CLI configuration file has the proper settings, you are ready to start using the SQLAlchemy module in your program to create persistent copies of Python program objects to be stored in Db2.

To learn more about SQLAlchemy, you should visit the www.sqlalchemy.org/ website.

The Alembic Adapter

The Alembic project is a subproject of the SQLAlchemy project. It is a migrations tool that allows the objects stored in an SQLAlchemy relational database to be migrated to another relational database. Whatever the reason may for using a different relational database than what is currently being used by you project, Alembic will allow you to migrate all your data to a new relational database, that is, migrate an SQLite SQLAlchemy database to Db2.

While this tool is not used on a daily basis in most environments, it is available when you need it.

To install the `ibm_db_alembic` module, use the following command:

```
sudo pip install ibm_db
sudo pip install ibm_db_alembic
```

This will install the latest version of the `ibm_db_alembic` and `ibm_db` modules on your machine.

To learn more about Alembic, you should visit the `https://alembic.sqlalchemy.org/` website.

The Future

The `ibm_db` module and its associated subprojects have made a really good start in allowing Python access to the Db2 environment. There are a number of possibilities for increasing this coverage, but at the time this book was written, there is one thing holding the new projects back – lack of developers. This is the same problem that prevents many open source projects from becoming all they could be. However, the `ibm_db` project has a slight advantage in that there is a small dedicated number of developers from IBM that are trying to move the project forward. But they need your help and support. So, if you have the time and inclination, please volunteer for the project.

Summary

In this chapter, we have introduced the `ibm_db` package and APIs. We have shown all the data manipulation SQL statements as well as many of the miscellaneous APIs. We have also introduced how to use parameter markers and the different ways that Python data can be bound to the statement that uses it.

Hopefully, the information and examples included in this chapter will give you a firm grasp on how you can use and manipulate a Db2 database. You also should be able to make better use of the Appendix information.

Python ibm_db API

This appendix documents the Python `ibm_db` API. The API is a part of a Python package that needs to be imported into your program. It consists of multiple function definitions that contain the API as methods of the class. In addition, there are also some functions defined as constants included in the package.

To include the ibm_db package, use the following Python code:

```
import ibm_db
```

This will make the entire API available to your Python program. It is a relatively small package, so importing all of it is really no imposition.

Much of the content of this chapter is taken from the GitHub website at

```
https://github.com.ibmdb/python-ibmdb/wiki/APIs
```

The major exception to this are the examples for each API. These have been totally replaced with examples that are runnable programs so that you can see how each API should be integrated in your own programs.

ibm_db APIs

All of the APIs documented in the following have at least one example included. All are complete programs so that it leaves no doubt about the way an API works.

ibm_db.active

```
bool ibm_db.active(IBM_DBConnection connection)
```

© W. David Ashley 2021
W. D. Ashley, *Foundation Db2 and Python*, https://doi.org/10.1007/978-1-4842-6942-8

Description

Determines if the IBM_DBConnection argument is active.

It returns either True if the connection is active or False if it is not.

Example

```
import ibm_db

dbstring = "DATABASE=dbname;HOSTNAME=host;PORT=port;PROTOCOL=TCPIP;UID=user
name;PWD=password"
conn=ibm_db.connect(dbstring, '', '')
connState = ibm_db.active(conn)
print(connState)
```

If you are running this on the local Db2 system, you do not need the PROTOCOL or the TCPIP parameter.

ibm_db.autocommit

```
mixed ibm_db.autocommit(IBM_DBConnection connection [, bool value])
```

Description

Returns and possibly sets the AUTOCOMMIT behavior of the connection argument. If the bool value argument is passed as ibm_db.SQL_AUTOCOMMIT_OFF or ibm_db.SQL_AUTOCOMMIT_ON, the return value will be either 0 if AUTOCOMMIT is off or 1 if AUTOCOMMIT is on.

If no bool value is passed, then the function returns True if AUTOCOMMIT was successfully set or False if AUTOCOMMIT was not set successfully.

Example

```
import ibm_db

options = {ibm_db.SQL_ATTR_AUTOCOMMIT:  ibm_db.SQL_AUTOCOMMIT_ON}
dbstring = "DATABASE=dbname;HOSTNAME=host;PORT=port;PROTOCOL=TCPIP;UID=user
name;PWD=password"
```

```
conn=ibm_db.connect(dbstring, '', '', options)
autocommitstatus = ibm_db.autocommit(conn)
print(autocommitstatus)
```

If you are running this on the local Db2 system, you do not need the PROTOCOL or the TCPIP parameter.

ibm_db.bind_param

```
bool ibm_db.bind_param (IBM_DBStatement stmt, int parameter-number, string variable \
[, int parameter-type [, int data-type [, int precision [, int scale [, int size]]]]])
```

Description

This function is a more powerful alternative to the ibm_db.execute() function. It binds a Python variable to an SQL statement parameter giving more control over the parameter type, data type, precision, and scale than simply passing the variable to the ibm_db.execute() as a tuple.

Parameters

- stmt: A prepared IBM_DBStatement statement returned from the ibm_db.prepare() function

- parameter-number: The 1-indexed position of the parameter in the prepared statement

- variable: A Python variable to be bound to the parameter specified by parameter-number

- parameter-type (optional): A constant specifying the parameter input/output type:

  - ibm_db.SQL_PARAM_INPUT: The Python variable is an input-only parameter.

  - ibm_db.SQL_PARAM_OUTPUT: The Python variable is an output-only parameter.

- • ibm_db.SQL_PARAM_INPUT_OUTPUT: The Python variable parameter is used for both input and output.

- • ibm_db.PARAM_FILE: The Python variable data is stored in the file specified in variable instead of in variable itself. This can be used to avoid storing lots of LOB data in memory.

- • data-type (optional): One of the following constants that indicate the data type of the Python variable data:

  - • ibm_db.SQL_BINARY

  - • ibm_db.DB2_CHAR

  - • ibm_db.DB2_DOUBLE

  - • ibm_db.DB2_LONG

- • precision (optional): The precision of a decimal Python variable

- • scale (optional): The scale of a decimal Python variable

Return Values

Returns True if the bind was successful and otherwise returns None.

Example

```
import ibm_db

dbstring = "DATABASE=dbname;HOSTNAME=host;PORT=port;PROTOCOL=TCPIP;UID=user
name;PWD=password"
conn=ibm_db.connect(dbstring, '', '', '')
stmt=ibm_db.prepare(conn, "select * from tabmany where id=?")
id=1
ibm_db.bind_param(stmt, 1, id)
ibm_db.execute(stmt)
row=ibm_db.fetch_tuple(stmt)
print(row)
```

If you are running this on the local Db2 system, you do not need the PROTOCOL or the TCPIP parameter.

ibm_db.callproc

(IBM_DBStatement [, ...]) ibm_db.callproc(IBM_DBConnection connection, string procname [, \ parameters])

Description

Calls a stored procedure stored under the given name. The parameter tuples must contain one entry for each argument (IN/OUT/INOUT) that the procedure expects. The function returns an IBM_DBStatement containing result sets and a possible modified copy of the input parameters. IN parameters are left untouched, whereas INOUT/OUT parameters are possibly replaced by new values.

A call to a stored procedure may return zero or more result sets. You can retrieve a row as a tuple/dict from the IBM_DBStatement using ibm_db.fetch_assoc(), ibm_db.fetch_both(), or ibm_db.fetch_tuple(). Alternatively, you can use ibm_db.fetch_row() to move the result set pointer to the next row and fetch a column at a time with ibm_db.result().

The parameters to the function include a valid IBM_DBConnection, a valid stored procedure name, and a possible set of zero or more sets of Python tuples which contain as many parameters as the stored procedure requires.

The function returns either a Python tuple containing an IBM_DBStatement object followed by the needed parameters for the procedure or an IBM_DBStatement object if there are no parameters passed to the procedure. On failure, it returns the Python value None.

Example

```
import ibm_db

dbstring = "DATABASE=dbname;HOSTNAME=host;PORT=port;PROTOCOL=TCPIP;UID=user
name;PWD=password"
conn=ibm_db.connect(dbstring, '', '', '')

sql = "create or replace procedure proc(OUT out1 integer) dynamic result
sets 1 "
sql += "begin select id into out1 from tabmany where id=1; end"
ibm_db.exec_immediate(conn, sql)
```

```
out1 = 0
stmt, out1 = ibm_db.callproc(conn,'proc',(out1,))
print(out1)

proc2 = "CREATE PROCEDURE out_blob(IN P1 BLOB(100),OUT P2 BLOB(100)) "
proc2 += "LANGUAGE SQL DYNAMIC RESULT SETS 0 BEGIN SET P2 = P1; END"""
result = ibm_db.exec_immediate(conn, proc2)
stmt, blob1, blob2 = ibm_db.callproc(conn, 'out_blob', (b'1234',b'0'))

if stmt is not None:
    print("Values of bound parameters _after_ CALL:")
    print("  1: %s\t 2: %s \n" % (blob1, blob2))
```

If you are running this on the local Db2 system, you do not need the PROTOCOL or the TCPIP parameter.

ibm_db.client_info

```
object ibm_db.client_info(IBM_DBConnection connection)
```

Description

Returns a read-only Python object with information about the database client. A valid IBM_DBConnection is the only required parameter.

Return Values

On success, an object has the following fields:

- APPL_CODEPAGE: The application code page used by the database.

- CONN_CODEPAGE: The code page for the current connection to the client.

- DATA_SOURCE_NAME: The data source name (DSN) used to create the current connection to the database.

- DRIVER_NAME: The name of the library that implements the Call-Level Interface (CLI) specification.

- DRIVER_ODBC_VER: The version of ODBC that the IBM data server client supports. This returns a string "MM.mm" where MM is the major version and mm is the minor version. The IBM data server client currently always returns "03.51".

- DRIVER_VER: The version of the client, in the form of a string "MM.mm.uuuu" where MM is the major version, mm is the minor version, and uuuu is the update. For example, "08.02.0001" represents major version 8, minor version 2, and update 1.

- ODBC_SQL_CONFORMANCE: There are three levels of ODBC SQL grammar supported by the Python client. This field will contain one of the following values:

  - MINIMAL: Supports the minimum ODBC SQL grammar.

  - CORE: Supports the core ODBC SQL grammar.

  - EXTENDED: Supports the extended ODBC SQL grammar.

- ODBC_VER: The version of ODBC that the ODBC driver manager supports. This returns a string "MM.mm.rrrr" where MM is the major version, mm is the minor version, and rrrr is the release. The client currently always returns "03.01.0000".

On failure, returns False.

Example

```
import ibm_db

dbstring = "DATABASE=dbname;HOSTNAME=host;PORT=port;PROTOCOL=TCPIP;UID=user
name;PWD=password"
conn=ibm_db.connect(dbstring, '', '', '')
client = ibm_db.client_info(conn)
if client:
    print("DRIVER_NAME: string(%d) \"%s\"" % (len(client.DRIVER_NAME),
    client.DRIVER_NAME))
    print("DRIVER_VER: string(%d) \"%s\"" % (len(client.DRIVER_VER),
    client.DRIVER_VER))
```

```
print("DATA_SOURCE_NAME: string(%d) \"%s\"" % (len(client.DATA_SOURCE_
NAME), client.DATA_SOURCE_NAME))
print("DRIVER_ODBC_VER: string(%d) \"%s\"" % (len(client.DRIVER_ODBC_
VER), client.DRIVER_ODBC_VER))
print("ODBC_VER: string(%d) \"%s\"" % (len(client.ODBC_VER), client.
ODBC_VER))
print("ODBC_SQL_CONFORMANCE: string(%d) \"%s\"" % (len(client.ODBC_SQL_
CONFORMANCE), client.ODBC_SQL_CONFORMANCE))
print("APPL_CODEPAGE: int(%s)" % client.APPL_CODEPAGE)
print("CONN_CODEPAGE: int(%s)" % client.CONN_CODEPAGE)
```

If you are running this on the local Db2 system, you do not need the PROTOCOL or the TCPIP parameter.

ibm_db.close

```
bool ibm_db.close(IBM_DBConnection connection)
```

Description

Closes a Db2 client connection and returns the corresponding resources to the database server.

If you attempt to close a persistent Db2 client connection created with ibm_db.pconnect(), the connection is returned to the pool for the next caller of ibm_db.pconnect() to use. The only required parameter is a valid IBM_DBConnection.

The function returns True on success or False on failure.

Example

```
import ibm_db

dbstring = "DATABASE=dbname;HOSTNAME=host;PORT=port;PROTOCOL=TCPIP;UID=user
name;PWD=password"
conn=ibm_db.connect(dbstring, '', '', '')

rc = ibm_db.close(conn)
print(rc)
```

If you are running this on the local Db2 system, you do not need the PROTOCOL or the TCPIP parameter.

ibm_db.column_privileges

```
IBM_DBStatement ibm_db.column_privileges (IBM_DBConnection connection
[, string qualifier [, string schema [, string table-name [, string
column-name]]]])
```

Description

Returns a result set listing the columns and associated privileges for a table.

There is one required parameter that is a valid IBM_DBConnection. The optional parameters include a Db2 qualifier for mainframe databases, a schema that contains the tables, a table-name that can be either a table or a view, and a column-name or None.

Return Values

An IBM_DBStatement result set containing rows with the following columns:

- TABLE_CAT: Name of the catalog. The value is None if the database does not have catalogs.

- TABLE_SCHEM: Name of the schema.

- TABLE_NAME: Name of the table or view.

- COLUMN_NAME: Name of the column.

- GRANTOR: Authorization ID of the user who granted the privilege.

- GRANTEE: Authorization ID of the user to whom the privilege was granted.

- PRIVILEGE: The privilege for the column.

- IS_GRANTABLE: Whether the GRANTEE is permitted to grant this privilege to other users.

Example

```
import ibm_db

dbstring = "DATABASE=dbname;HOSTNAME=host;PORT=port;PROTOCOL=TCPIP;UID=user
name;PWD=password"
conn=ibm_db.connect(dbstring, '', '', '')

# ANIMAL is the table name
stmt = ibm_db.column_privileges(conn, None, None, 'ANIMALS')
row = ibm_db.fetch_tuple(stmt)
if row:
    print(row[0])
    print(row[1])
    print(row[2])
    print(row[3])
    print(row[4])
    print(row[5])
    print(row[6])
    print(row[7])

ibm_db.close(conn)
```

If you are running this on the local Db2 system, you do not need the PROTOCOL or the TCPIP parameter.

ibm_db.columns

IBM_DBStatement ibm_db.columns (IBM_DBConnection connection [, string qualifier [, string schema [, string table-name [, string column-name]]]])

Description

Returns a result set listing the columns and associated metadata for a table.

Parameters

- `Connection`: A valid `IBM_DBConnection`

- `qualifier` (optional): A qualifier for Db2 databases running on OS/390 or z/OS servers. For other databases, pass None or an empty string.

- `schema` (optional): The schema that contains the tables. To match all schemas, pass the string '%'.

- `table-name` (optional): The name of the table or view. To match all tables in the database, pass None or an empty string.

- `column-name` (optional): The name of the column. To match all columns in the table, pass None or an empty string.

Return Values

An `IBM_DBStatement` with a result set containing rows containing the following columns:

- `TABLE_CAT`: Name of the catalog. The value is None if this table does not have catalogs.

- `TABLE_SCHEM`: Name of the schema.

- `TABLE_NAME` :Name of the table or view.

- `COLUMN_NAME`: Name of the column.

- `DATA_TYPE`: The SQL data type for the column represented as an integer value.

- `TYPE_NAME`: A string representing the data type for the column.

- `COLUMN_SIZE`: An integer value representing the size of the column in bytes.

- `BUFFER_LENGTH`: Maximum number of bytes necessary to store data from this column.

- `DECIMAL_DIGITS`: The scale of the decimal column, or None where scale is not applicable for the column.

- NUM_PREC_RADIX: An integer value of either 10 (representing an exact numeric data type), 2 (representing an approximate numeric data type), or None (representing a data type for which radix is not applicable for the column).

- NULLABLE: An integer value representing whether the column is nullable or not.

- REMARKS: Description of the column.

- COLUMN_DEF: Default value for the column when inserting/altering the column.

- SQL_DATA_TYPE: The SQL data type of the column.

- SQL_DATETIME_SUB: An integer value representing a datetime subtype code, or None for SQL data types to which this does not apply to the column.

- CHAR_OCTET_LENGTH: Maximum length in octets for a character data type column, which matches COLUMN_SIZE for single-byte character set data or None for non-character data types.

- ORDINAL_POSITION: The 1-indexed position of the column in the table.

- IS_NULLABLE: A string value where 'YES' means that the column is nullable and 'NO' means that the column is not nullable.

Example

```
import ibm_db

dbstring = "DATABASE=dbname;HOSTNAME=host;PORT=port;PROTOCOL=TCPIP;UID=user
name;PWD=password"
conn=ibm_db.connect(dbstring, '', '', '')

# TABMANY is table name
result = ibm_db.columns(conn,None,None,"TABMANY")
row = ibm_db.fetch_both(result)
```

```
if row:
    table_name=row['TABLE_NAME']
    column_name=row['COLUMN_NAME']
print("Table name              : {}" .format(table_name))
print("column name             : {}" .format(column_name))
```

If you are running this on the local Db2 system, you do not need the PROTOCOL or the TCPIP parameter.

ibm_db.commit

```
bool ibm_db.commit (IBM_DBConnection connection)
```

Description

Commits an in-progress transaction on the specified IBM_DBConnection and begins a new transaction.

Python applications normally default to AUTOCOMMIT mode, so ibm_db.commit() is not necessary unless AUTOCOMMIT has been turned off for the IBM_DBConnection.

One IBM_DBConnection parameter is required by the function.

The function returns True on success or False on failure.

Note   If the specified IBM_DBConnection is a persistent connection, all transactions in progress for all applications using that persistent connection will be committed. For this reason, persistent connections are not recommended for use in applications that require transactions.

Example

```
import ibm_db

dbstring = "DATABASE=dbname;HOSTNAME=host;PORT=port;PROTOCOL=TCPIP;UID=user
name;PWD=password"
conn=ibm_db.connect(dbstring, '', '', '')
```

```
#set autocommit off
rc = ibm_db.autocommit(conn, ibm_db.SQL_AUTOCOMMIT_OFF)

#insert a row
stmt = ibm_db.exec_immediate(conn, "insert into tabmany values(2, 'commit
test')")

#commit the transaction explicitly as autocommit is off
rc = ibm_db.commit(conn)

#validate that row is inserted
sql_stmt = ibm_db.exec_immediate(conn, "select * from tabmany")
row = ibm_db.fetch_tuple(sql_stmt)
if row:
    print(str(row[0]) + "\n" + row[1])

#close the connection
ibm_db.close(conn)
```

If you are running this on the local Db2 system, you do not need the PROTOCOL or the TCPIP parameter.

ibm_db.conn_error

```
string ibm_db.conn_error ([IBM_DBConnection connection])
```

Description

When no parameters are passed, returns the SQLSTATE representing the reason the last database connection attempt failed.

When passed a valid IBM_DBConnection returned by ibm_db.connect(), returns the SQLSTATE representing the reason the last operation using an IBM_DBConnection failed.

The function requires a valid IBM_DBConnection parameter and returns a string containing the SQLSTATE value or an empty string if there was no error.

Example

```
import ibm_db

#try connecting with an invalid user name
try:
    dbstring = "DATABASE=dbname;HOSTNAME=host;PORT=port;PROTOCOL=TCPIP;
    UID=uname;PWD=password"
    conn=ibm_db.connect(dbstring, '', '', '')
except:
    print("Error in connection, sqlstate = ")
    errorState = ibm_db.conn_error()
    print(errorState)
```

ibm_db.conn_errormsg

```
string ibm_db.conn_errormsg ([IBM_DBConnection connection])
```

Description

When no parameters are passed, returns a string containing the SQLCODE and error message representing the reason the last database connection attempt failed.

When passed a valid IBM_DBConnection returned by ibm_db.connect(), returns a string containing the SQLCODE and error message representing the reason the last operation using an IBM_DBConnection failed.

Example

```
import ibm_db

#try connecting with an invalid user name
try:
    dbstring = "DATABASE=dbname;HOSTNAME=host;PORT=port;PROTOCOL=TCPIP;
    UID=xxx;PWD=password"
    conn=ibm_db.connect(dbstring, '', '', '')
```

```
except:
    print("Error in connection, sqlstate = ")
    errorMsg = ibm_db.conn_errormsg()
    print(errorMsg)
```

If you are running this on the local Db2 system, you do not need the PROTOCOL or the TCPIP parameter.

ibm_db.connect

IBM_DBConnection ibm_db.connect(string database, string user, string password , [dict options [, constant replace_quoted_literal]])

Description

Creates a new connection to an IBM Db2 Universal Database, IBM Cloudscape, or Apache Derby database.

Parameters

- database: For a catalogued connection to a database, this parameter represents the database alias in the Db2 client catalog. For an uncatalogued connection to a database, represents a complete connection string in the following format, DRIVER={IBM DB2 ODBCD RIVER};DATABASE=database;HOSTNAME=hostname;PORT=port; PRO TOCOL=TCPIP;UID=username;PWD=password; where the parameters represent the following values:

  - hostname: The hostname or IP address of the database server

  - Port: The TCP/IP port on which the database is listening for requests

  - Username: The username with which you are connecting to the database

  - Password: The password with which you are connecting to the database

- user: The username with which you are connecting to the database. For uncatalogued connections, you must pass an empty string.

- password: The password of the user with which you are connecting to the database. For uncatalogued connections, you must pass an empty string.

- options (optional): A dict of connection options that affect the behavior of the connection:

  - SQL_ATTR_AUTOCOMMIT: Either SQL_AUTOCOMMIT_ON or SQL_AUTOCOMMIT_OFF.

  - ATTR_CASE: Either CASE_NATURAL, CASE_LOWER, or CASEUPPER.

  - SQL_ATTR_CURSOR_TYPE: Either SQL_CURSOR_FORWARD_ONLY, SQL_CURSOR_KEYSET_DRIVEN, SQL_CURSOR_DYNAMIC, or SQL_CURSOR_STATIC.

  - SQL_ATTR_INFO_PROGRAMNAME: A null-terminated user-defined character string, up to 20 bytes in length. Used to specify the name of the application running on the client.

  - SQL_ATTR_USE_TRUSTED_CONTEXT: When connecting to a Db2 database server that supports trusted contexts. Set this attribute if you want the connection you are creating to be a trusted connection.

  - SQL_ATTR_TRUSTED_CONTEXT_USERID: A user-defined string containing a user ID. Use this on existing trusted connections to switch users. Do not use it when creating a trusted connection.

  - SQL_ATTR_TRUSTED_CONTEXT_PASSWORD: A user-defined string containing a password. Use this attribute if the database server requires a password when switching users on a trusted connection. Set this attribute after setting the attribute SQL_ATTR_TRUSTED_CONTEXT_USERID and before executing any SQL statement that accesses the database server.

- • SQL_ATTR_CURRENT_SCHEMA: A character string containing the name of the schema to be used by CLI for the SQLColumns() call if the szSchemaName pointer is set to null. Refer to ibm_db.columns for an example.

- • SQL_ATTR_INFO_USERID: The SQL_ATTR_INFO_USERID attribute is used to set the client user ID (accounting user ID) that is sent to a database. The SQL_ATTR_INFO_USERID attribute is for identification purposes only and is not used for any authentication. Do not confuse the SQL_ATTR_INFO_USERID attribute with the authentication user ID. The CLI driver has a limit of 255 characters for the SQL_ATTR_INFO_USERID attribute.

- • SQL_ATTR_INFO_WRKSTNNAME: The SQL_ATTR_INFO_WRKSTNNAME attribute is used to set the client workstation name that is sent to a database. The CLI driver has a limit of 255 characters for the SQL_ATTR_INFO_WRKSTNNAME attribute.

- • SQL_ATTR_INFO_ACCTSTR: The SQL_ATTR_INFO_ACCTSTR attribute is used to set the client accounting string that is sent to a database. The CLI driver has a limit of 255 characters for the SQL_ATTR_INFO_ACCTSTR attribute.

- • SQL_ATTR_INFO_APPLNAME: The SQL_ATTR_INFO_APPLNAME attribute is used to set the client application name that is sent to a database. The CLI driver has a limit of 255 characters for the SQL_ATTR_INFO_APPLNAME attribute.

- • replace_quoted_literal: Indicates if the CLI connection attribute SQL_ATTR_REPLACE_QUOTED_LITERAL is to be set or not. Either QUOTED_LITERAL_REPLACEMENT_ON or QUOTED_LITERAL_REPLACEMENT_OFF.

For more information on these keywords, please refer to IBM data server driver configuration keywords.

Return Values

On success, an IBM_DBConnection object; on failure, None.

Example 1

```
import ibm_db
#use connection string
dbstring = "DATABASE=dbname;HOSTNAME=host;PORT=port;PROTOCOL=TCPIP;UID=user
name;PWD=password"

#use options
options = {ibm_db.SQL_ATTR_INFO_PROGRAMNAME : 'TestProgram', \
           ibm_db.SQL_ATTR_CURRENT_SCHEMA : 'MYSCHEMA'}
conn=ibm_db.connectdbstring,'','', options)
```

If you are running this on the local Db2 system, you do not need the PROTOCOL or the
TCPIP parameter.

Sample Configuration in db2dsdriver.cfg

```
<configuration>
   <dsncollection>
      <dsn alias="sampledb" name="sample" host="www.example.com"
      port="50000">
      </dsn>
   </dsncollection>
   <databases>
      <database name="sample" host="www.example.com" port="50000">
         <parameter name="userid" value="username"/>
         <parameter name="password" value="xxxxxx"/>
      </database>
   </databases>
</configuration>
```

ibm_db.createdb

```
bool ibm_db.createdb(IBM_DBConnection connection, string dbName [, codeSet,
mode])
```

Description

Creates a database by using the specified connection, database name, codeSet, and mode. The function returns True if the database was created successfully or None if there was an error.

Example

```
import ibm_db
dbstring = "DATABASE=dbname;HOSTNAME=host;PORT=port;PROTOCOL=TCPIP;UID=user
name;PWD=password"
conn=ibm_db.connect(dbstring, '', '', '')
database='test123'
conn_attach = ibm_db.connect(conn_str_attach, '', '')
rc = ibm_db.createdb(conn_attach, database)
```

If you are running this on the local Db2 system, you do not need the PROTOCOL or the TCPIP parameter.

ibm_db.createdbNX

```
bool ibm_db.createdbNX(IBM_DBConnection connection, string dbName [,
codeSet, mode])
```

Description

Creates the database if it does not exist by using the specified connection, database dbName, codeSet, and mode.

Returns True if the database was created successfully or None if there was an error.

Example

```
import ibm_db

database='test123'
dbstring = "DATABASE=dbname;HOSTNAME=host;PORT=port;PROTOCOL=TCPIP;UID=user
name;PWD=password"
conn=ibm_db.connect(dbstring, '', '', '')
rc = ibm_db.createdbNX(conn_attach, database) ibm_db.cursor_type
```

If you are running this on the local Db2 system, you do not need the PROTOCOL or the TCPIP parameter.

ibm_db.cursor_type

```
int ibm_db.cursor_type(IBM_DBStatement stmt)
```

Description

Returns the cursor type used by an IBM_DBStatement. Use this to determine if you are working with a forward-only cursor or scrollable cursor. The only required parameter is an IBM DBConnection.

Return Values

- One of the following constant values: SQL_CURSOR_FORWARD_ONLY, SQL_CURSOR_KEYSET_DRIVEN, SQL_CURSOR_DYNAMIC, or SQL_CURSOR_STATIC

Example

```
import ibm_db

dbstring = "DATABASE=dbname;HOSTNAME=host;PORT=port;PROTOCOL=TCPIP;UID=user
name;PWD=password"
conn = ibm_db.connect(dbstring, '', '', '')

stmtOption = {ibm_db.SQL_ATTR_CURSOR_TYPE: ibm_db.SQL_CURSOR_FORWARD_ONLY}
sqlStatement = "SELECT * FROM tabmany"
resultSet = ibm_db.exec_immediate(conn, sqlStatement, stmtOption)

#get the cursor type
cursorType = ibm_db.cursor_type(resultSet)
```

If you are running this on the local Db2 system, you do not need the PROTOCOL or the TCPIP parameter.

ibm_db.dropdb

```
bool ibm_db.dropdb(IBM_DBConnection connection, string dbName)
```

Description

Drops the specified database. The required parameters are an IBM_DBConnection and the name of the database dbname.

The function returns True if the database was dropped successfully or None if there was a problem.

Example

```
import ibm_db

dbstring = "DATABASE=dbname;HOSTNAME=host;PORT=port;PROTOCOL=TCPIP;UID=user
name;PWD=password"
conn = ibm_db.connect(dbstring, '', '', '')

dbName = "MY_DB"
rc = ibm_db.dropdb(conn, dbName)
```

If you are running this on the local Db2 system, you do not need the PROTOCOL or the TCPIP parameter.

ibm_db.exec_immediate

```
stmt_handle ibm_db.exec_immediate(IBM_DBConnection connection, string
statement [, dict options])
```

Description

Prepares and executes an SQL statement.

If you plan to repeatedly issue the same SQL statement with different parameters, consider calling ibm_db.prepare() and ibm_db.execute() to enable the database server to reuse its access plan and increase the efficiency of your database access.

If you plan to interpolate Python variables into the SQL statement, understand that this statement is one of the more common security exposures. Consider calling `ibm_db.prepare()` to prepare an SQL statement with parameter markers for input values. Then you can call `ibm_db.execute()` to pass in the input values and avoid SQL injection attacks.

Parameters

- `Connection`: A valid `IBM_DBConnection`.

- `statement`: An SQL statement. The statement cannot contain any parameter markers.

- `options` (optional): A Python `dict` containing one of the following statement options:

  - SQL_ATTR_CURSOR_TYPE: Set the cursor type to one of the following (not supported on all databases):

    - SQL_CURSOR_FORWARD_ONLY

    - SQL_CURSOR_KEYSET_DRIVEN

    - SQL_CURSOR_DYNAMIC

    - SQL_CURSOR_STATIC

Return Values

Returns a `stmt_handle` resource if the SQL statement was issued successfully or `False` if the database failed to execute the SQL statement.

Example

```
import ibm_db
import pandas as pd
import ibm_db_dbi as dbi

dbstring = "DATABASE=dbname;HOSTNAME=host;PORT=port;PROTOCOL=TCPIP;UID=user
name;PWD=password"
conn = ibm_db.connect(dbstring, '', '', '')
```

```
sql_stmt =  "select * from tabmany"
result = ibm_db.exec_immediate(conn, sql_stmt)
if stmt is not None:
    row = ibm_db.fetch_tuple(result)
    while(row):
        print("{}\t{}\n".format(row[0],row[1])
        row = ibm_db.fetch_tuple(result)

# use pandas dataframe
conn1 = dbi.connect(dbstring)
df = pd.read_sql("select * from tabmany", conn1)
print(df)
```

If you are running this on the local Db2 system, you do not need the PROTOCOL or the TCPIP parameter.

ibm_db.execute

```
bool ibm_db.execute(IBM_DBStatement stmt [, tuple parameters])
```

Description

ibm_db.execute() executes an SQL statement that was prepared by ibm_db.prepare(). If the SQL statement returns a result set, for example, a SELECT statement that returns one or more result sets, you can retrieve a row as a tuple/dict from the stmt resource using ibm_db.fetch_assoc(), ibm_db.fetch_both(), or ibm_db.fetch_tuple(). Alternatively, you can use ibm_db.fetch_row() to move the result set pointer to the next row and fetch a column at a time from that row with ibm_db.result(). Refer to ibm_db.prepare() for a brief discussion of the advantages of using ibm_db.prepare() and ibm_db.execute() rather than ibm_db.exec_immediate(). To execute stored procedures, refer to ibm_db.callproc().

This function has one required IBM_DBStatement parameter and multiple optional parameters that are Python tuples matching the parameter markers contained in the stmt.

The return value is True on success and False on failure.

Example

```
import ibm_db

dbstring = "DATABASE=dbname;HOSTNAME=host;PORT=port;PROTOCOL=TCPIP;UID=user
name;PWD=password"
conn = ibm_db.connect(dbstring, '', '', '')

sql_stmt = "insert into tabmany values(?,?)"
stmt = ibm_db.prepare(conn, sql_stmt)
id = 3
name = "Sam"
ibm_db.bind_param(stmt, 1, id)
ibm_db.bind_param(stmt, 2, name)
try:
    ibm_db.execute(stmt)
except:
    print(ibm_db.stmt_errormsg())
```

If you are running this on the local Db2 system, you do not need the PROTOCOL or the TCPIP parameter.

ibm_db.execute_many

```
mixed ibm_db.execute_many(IBM_DBStatement stmt, tuple seq_of_parameters)
```

Description

Executes an SQL statement prepared by the ibm_db.prepare() function against all parameter sequences or mappings found in the sequence seq_of_parameters. Use this function for bulk insert/update/delete operations. It uses the ArrayInputChaining feature of Db2 CLI to ensure minimum roundtrips to the server.

This function requires two parameters. The first is an SQL stmt, and the second is a Python tuple of tuples, which are contained in the SQL stmt.

On success, the function returns the number of rows processed and on failure returns None.

Example

```
import ibm_db
import ibm_db_dbi as dbi
import pandas as pd

dbstring = "DATABASE=dbname;HOSTNAME=host;PORT=port;PROTOCOL=TCPIP;UID=user
name;PWD=password"
conn = ibm_db.connect(dbstring, '', '', '')

ibm_db.exec_immediate(conn,"CREATE table tabmany( id SMALLINT , name
VARCHAR(32))")
insert = "insert into tabmany values(?,?)"
values=(1,'sample')
params=tuple(tuple (x+i if type(x)==int else x+str(i) for x in values) for
i in range(3))
stmt_insert = ibm_db.prepare(conn, insert)
ibm_db.execute_many(stmt_insert,params)
row_count = ibm_db.num_rows(stmt_insert)
print("inserted {} rows".format(row_count))

# use data frame, requires ibm_db_dbi connection
dbstring = "DATABASE=dbname;HOSTNAME=host;PORT=port;PROTOCOL=TCPIP;UID=user
name;PWD=password"
conn1 = ibm_db.connect(dbstring, '', '', '')

data={'ID':[11,22,33,44],'NAME':['val1','val2','val3','val4']}
df1=pd.DataFrame(data)
tuple_of_tuples = tuple([tuple(x) for x in df1.values])
sql="insert into testmany values(?,?)"

stmt=ibm_db.prepare(conn,sql)
ibm_db.execute_many(stmt,tuple_of_tuples)

df2=pd.read_sql("select * from test",conn1)
print(df2)
```

```
subset = df2[['ID','NAME','RATING']]
tuple_of_tuples1 = tuple([tuple(x) for x in subset.values])
ibm_db.execute_many(stmt,tuple_of_tuples1)

df3=pd.read_sql("select * from test", conn1)
print(df3)
```

If you are running this on the local Db2 system, you do not need the PROTOCOL or the TCPIP parameter.

ibm_db.fetch_tuple

```
tuple ibm_db.fetch_tuple(IBM_DBStatement stmt [, int row_number])
```

Description

Returns a tuple, indexed by column position, representing a row in a result set.

This function has one required parameter that is a valid SQL stmt and one optional parameter that limits the returned Python tuple to a single row specified by the row_number. The function returns a single row as a tuple containing al the column values.

If row_number is specified, it returns that row information; otherwise, it returns the next row. If an error occurs, it returns False.

Example

```
import ibm_db

dbstring = "DATABASE=dbname;HOSTNAME=host;PORT=port;PROTOCOL=TCPIP;UID=user
name;PWD=password"
conn = ibm_db.connect(dbstring, '', '', '')

sql = "select id, name from tabmany"
stmt = ibm_db.exec_immediate(conn, sql)

row = ibm_db.fetch_tuple(stmt)
while ( row ):
```

```
    for i in row:
        print(i)
    row = ibm_db.fetch_tuple(stmt)
ibm_db.close(conn)
```

If you are running this on the local Db2 system, you do not need the PROTOCOL or the TCPIP parameter.

ibm_db.fetch_assoc

```
dict ibm_db.fetch_assoc(IBM_DBStatement stmt [, int row_number])
```

Description

Returns a dict, indexed by column name, representing a row in a result set.

This function has one required parameter that is a valid SQL stmt and one optional parameter that limits the returned Python dict to a single row specified by the row_number. The function returns a single row as a dict containing all the column values.

If row_number is specified, it returns that row information; otherwise, it returns the next row. If an error occurs, it returns False.

Example

```
import ibm_db

dbstring = "DATABASE=dbname;HOSTNAME=host;PORT=port;PROTOCOL=TCPIP;UID=user
name;PWD=password"
conn=ibm_db.connect(dbstring, '', '', '')

sql = "select id, name from tabmany"
stmt = ibm_db.prepare(conn, sql,{ibm_db.SQL_ATTR_CURSOR_TYPE: ibm_db.SQL_
CURSOR_KEYSET_DRIVEN})
result = ibm_db.execute(stmt)
#fetch every alternate row starting from 2nd
i = 2
row = ibm_db.fetch_assoc(stmt, i)
while ( row ):
```

```
print("%-5d %-16s " % (row['ID'], row['NAME']))
i = i + 2
row = ibm_db.fetch_assoc(stmt, i)
```

If you are running this on the local Db2 system, you do not need the PROTOCOL or the TCPIP parameter .

ibm_db.fetch_both

```
dict ibm_db.fetch_both(IBM_DBStatement stmt [, int row_number])
```

Description

Returns a dict, indexed by column name and position, representing a row in a result set.

This function has one required parameter that is a valid SQL stmt and one optional parameter that limits the returned Python dict to a single row specified by the row_number. The function returns a single row as a dict containing all the column values.

If row_number is specified, it returns that row information: otherwise, it returns the next row. If an error occurs, it returns False.

Example

```
import ibm_db

dbstring = "DATABASE=dbname;HOSTNAME=host;PORT=port;PROTOCOL=TCPIP;UID=user
name;PWD=password"
conn = ibm_db.connect(dbstring, '', '', '')

sql = "select id, name from tabmany"
stmt = ibm_db.prepare(conn, sql,)
result = ibm_db.execute(stmt)
row = ibm_db.fetch_both(stmt)
while ( row ):
    print("%-5d %-5d " % (row['ID'], row[0]))
    print("%-16s %-16s " % (row['NAME'], row[1]))
    row = ibm_db.fetch_both(stmt)
```

If you are running this on the local Db2 system, you do not need the PROTOCOL or the TCPIP parameter.

ibm_db.fetch_row

```
bool ibm_db.fetch_row(IBM_DBStatement stmt [, int row_number])
```

Description

Sets the result set pointer to the next row or requested row.

Use ibm_db.fetch_row() to iterate through a result set or to point to a specific row in a result set if you requested a scrollable cursor.

To retrieve individual fields (columns) from the result set, call the ibm_db.result() function. Rather than calling ibm_db.fetch_row() and ibm_db.result(), most applications will call one of ibm_db.fetch_assoc(), ibm_db.fetch_both(), or ibm_db.fetch_tuple() to advance the result set pointer and return a complete row.

This function has one required parameter that is a valid SQL stmt. It also has one optional parameter that specifies the row_number to be fetched.

It returns True if the requested row exists in the result set; otherwise, it returns False.

Example

```python
import ibm_db

dbstring = "DATABASE=dbname;HOSTNAME=host;PORT=port;PROTOCOL=TCPIP;UID=user
name;PWD=password"
conn = ibm_db.connect(dbstring, '', '', '')

sql = "select id, name from tabmany"
stmt = ibm_db.prepare(conn, sql,)
result = ibm_db.execute(stmt)
row = ibm_db.fetch_row(stmt)
while ( row ):
    print(row)
    row = ibm_db.fetch_row(stmt)
```

If you are running this on the local Db2 system, you do not need the PROTOCOL or the TCPIP parameter.

ibm_db.field_display_size

```
int ibm_db.field_display_size(IBM_DBStatement stmt, mixed column)
```

Description

Returns the maximum number of bytes required to display a column in a result set.

This function requires two parameters, an SQL stmt and a 0-indexed position of the column or the name of the column.

The function returns an integer representing the number of bytes required to display the largest column value. If there was an error, False is returned.

Example

```
import ibm_db

dbstring = "DATABASE=dbname;HOSTNAME=host;PORT=port;PROTOCOL=TCPIP;UID=user
name;PWD=password"
conn = ibm_db.connect(dbstring, '', '', '')

sql = "select id, name from tabmany"
stmt = ibm_db.prepare(conn, sql,)
result = ibm_db.execute(stmt)
cols = ibm_db.num_fields(stmt)
for i in range(0, cols):
    size = ibm_db.field_display_size(stmt,i)
    print("col:%d and size: %d" % (i, size))
```

If you are running this on the local Db2 system, you do not need the PROTOCOL or the TCPIP parameter.

ibm_db.field_name

```
string ibm_db.field_name(IBM_DBStatement stmt, mixed column)
```

Description

Returns the name of the specified column in the result set.

The function requires two parameters. The first is the SQL stmt and the second is the 0-indexed position of the column or the name of the column.

The function returns the name of the column or False if there was an error.

Example

```
import ibm_db

dbstring = "DATABASE=dbname;HOSTNAME=host;PORT=port;PROTOCOL=TCPIP;UID=user
name;PWD=password"
conn = ibm_db.connect(dbstring, '', '', '')

sql = "select id, name from tabmany"
field_name=[]
stmt = ibm_db.prepare(conn, sql,)
result = ibm_db.execute(stmt)
cols = ibm_db.num_fields(stmt)
for i in range(0, cols):
    field_name.append(ibm_db.field_name(stmt,i))
print(field_name)
```

If you are running this on the local Db2 system, you do not need the PROTOCOL or the TCPIP parameter.

ibm_db.field_num

```
int ibm_db.field_num(IBM_DBStatement stmt, mixed column)
```

Description

Returns the position of the named column in a result set.

Parameters

- stmt: Specifies an IBM_DBStatement containing a result set. column: Specifies the column in the result set. This can either be an integer representing the 0-indexed position of the column or a string containing the name of the column.

The function requires two parameters. The first is the SQL stmt and the second is the 0-indexed position of the column or the name of the column.

The function returns the 0-indexed position of the column or False if there was an error.

Return Values

Returns an integer containing the 0-indexed position of the specified column or False if the column does not exist.

Example

```
import ibm_db

dbstring = "DATABASE=dbname;HOSTNAME=host;PORT=port;PROTOCOL=TCPIP;UID=user
name;PWD=password"
conn = ibm_db.connect(dbstring, '', '', '')

sql = "select id, name from tabmany"
field_num=[]
field_name=[]
stmt = ibm_db.prepare(conn, sql,)
result = ibm_db.execute(stmt)
cols = ibm_db.num_fields(stmt)

# index by column number
for i in range(0, cols):
    field_name.append(ibm_db.field_name(stmt,i))
    field_num.append(ibm_db.field_num(stmt,field_name[i]))
print(field_num)
```

```
# index by column name
field_num=[]
field_num.append(ibm_db.field_num(stmt, 'ID'))
field_num.append(ibm_db.field_num(stmt, 'NAME'))
print(field_num)
```

If you are running this on the local Db2 system, you do not need the PROTOCOL or the TCPIP parameter.

ibm_db.field_precision

```
int ibm_db.field_precision(IBM_DBStatement stmt, mixed column)
```

Description

Returns the precision of the indicated column in a result set.

The function requires two parameters. The first is the SQL stmt and the second is the 0-indexed position of the column or the name of the column.

The function returns the precision of the column or False if there was an error.

Example

```
import ibm_db

dbstring = "DATABASE=dbname;HOSTNAME=host;PORT=port;PROTOCOL=TCPIP;UID=user
name;PWD=password"
conn = ibm_db.connect(dbstring, '', '', '')

sql = "select id, name from tabmany"
field_precision=[]
stmt = ibm_db.prepare(conn, sql,)
result = ibm_db.execute(stmt)
cols = ibm_db.num_fields(stmt)
for i in range(0, cols):
    field_precision.append(ibm_db.field_precision(stmt,i))
print(field_precision)

row = ibm_db.fetch_tuple(stmt)
```

```
# use the precision to format the data display
print("{:<{prec}}\t{:>{char_prec}}". \
format(row[0],row[1],prec=field_precision[0],char_prec=field_precision[1]))
```

If you are running this on the local Db2 system, you do not need the PROTOCOL or the TCPIP parameter.

ibm_db.field_scale

```
int ibm_db.field_scale(IBM_DBStatement stmt, mixed column)
```

Description

Returns the scale of the indicated column in a result set.

The function requires two parameters. The first is the SQL stmt and the second is the 0-indexed position of the column or the name of the column.

The function returns the scale of the column or False if there was an error.

Example

```
import ibm_db

dbstring = "DATABASE=dbname;HOSTNAME=host;PORT=port;PROTOCOL=TCPIP;UID=user
name;PWD=password"
conn = ibm_db.connect(dbstring, '', '', '')

insert = "insert into scale_test values(25280.00, 17600.00)"
ibm_db.exec_immediate(conn, insert)

sql = "select salary, bonus from scale_test"
field_scale=[]
stmt = ibm_db.prepare(conn, sql)
result = ibm_db.execute(stmt)
cols = ibm_db.num_fields(stmt)
for i in range(0, cols):
    field_scale.append(ibm_db.field_scale(stmt,i))
print(field_scale)
```

```
row = ibm_db.fetch_tuple(stmt)
print("{:<{scale1}}\t{:>{scale2}}". \ format(row[0],row[1],scale1=field_
scale[0],scale2=field_scale[1]))
```

If you are running this on the local Db2 system, you do not need the PROTOCOL or the TCPIP parameter.

ibm_db.field_type

```
string ibm_db.field_type(IBM_DBStatement stmt, mixed column)
```

Description

Returns the data type of the indicated column in a result set.

The function requires two parameters. The first is the SQL stmt and the second is the 0-indexed position of the column or the name of the column.

The function returns the data type of the column as a string or False if there was an error.

Example

```
import ibm_db

dbstring = "DATABASE=dbname;HOSTNAME=host;PORT=port;PROTOCOL=TCPIP;UID=user
name;PWD=password"
conn = ibm_db.connect(dbstring, '', '', '')

result = ibm_db.exec_immediate(conn, "select * from tabmany")
for i in range(0, ibm_db.num_fields(result) ):
    print(str(i) + ":" + str(ibm_db.field_type(result,i)))
```

If you are running this on the local Db2 system, you do not need the PROTOCOL or the TCPIP parameter.

ibm_db.field_width

```
int ibm_db.field_width(IBM_DBStatement stmt, mixed column)
```

Description

Returns the width of the current value of the indicated column in a result set. This is the maximum width of the column for a fixed-length data type or the actual width of the column for a variable-length data type.

The function requires two parameters. The first is the SQL stmt and the second is the 0-indexed position of the column or the name of the column.

The function returns the field width of the column or False if there was an error.

Example

```
import ibm_db

dbstring = "DATABASE=dbname;HOSTNAME=host;PORT=port;PROTOCOL=TCPIP;UID=user
name;PWD=password"
conn = ibm_db.connect(dbstring, '', '', '')

result = ibm_db.exec_immediate(conn, "select * from tabmany")
for i in range(0, ibm_db.num_fields(result) ):
    col_width = ibm_db.field_width(result, i)
    col_name = ibm_db.field_name(result,i)
    #print(col_name,col_width)
    print("{:<{width}}".format(col_name, width=col_width),end=" ")
```

If you are running this on the local Db2 system, you do not need the PROTOCOL or the TCPIP parameter.

ibm_db.foreign_keys

```
IBM_DBStatement ibm_db.foreign_keys(IBM_DBConnection connection, string
pk_qualifier, string pk_schema, string pk_table-name, string fk_qualifier,
string fk_schema, string fk_table-name)
```

Description

Returns a result set listing the foreign keys for a table.

Parameters

- connection: A valid IBM_DBConnection

- pk_qualifier: A qualifier for the pk_table-name argument for the Db2 databases running on OS/390 or z/OS servers. For other databases, pass None or an empty string.

- pk_schema: The schema for the pk_table-name argument that contains the tables. If schema is None, the current schema for the connection is used instead.

- pk_table-name: The name of the table that contains the primary key.

- fk_qualifier: A qualifier for the fk_table-name argument for the Db2 databases running on OS/390 or z/OS servers. For other databases, pass None or an empty string.

- fk_schema: The schema for the fk_table-name argument that contains the tables. If schema is None, the current schema for the connection is used instead.

- fk_table-name: The name of the table that contains the foreign key.

Return Values

Returns an IBM_DBStatement with a result set containing the following columns:

- PKTABLE_CAT: Name of the catalog for the table containing the primary key. The value is None if this table does not have catalogs.

- PKTABLE_SCHEM: Name of the schema for the table containing the primary key.

- PKTABLE_NAME: Name of the table containing the primary key.

- PKCOLUMN_NAME: Name of the column containing the primary key.

- FKTABLE_CAT: Name of the catalog for the table containing the foreign key. The value is None if this table does not have catalogs.

- FKTABLE_SCHEM: Name of the schema for the table containing the foreign key.

- FKTABLE_NAME: Name of the table containing the foreign key.

- FKCOLUMN_NAME: Name of the column containing the foreign key.

- KEY_SEQ: 1-indexed position of the column in the key.

- UPDATE_RULE: Integer value representing the action applied to the foreign key when the SQL operation is UPDATE.

- DELETE_RULE: Integer value representing the action applied to the foreign key when the SQL operation is DELETE.

- FK_NAME: The name of the foreign key.

- PK_NAME: The name of the primary key.

- DEFERRABILITY: An integer value representing whether the foreign key deferrability is SQL_INITIALLY_DEFERRED, SQL_INITIALLY_ IMMEDIATE, or SQL_NOT_DEFERRABLE.

If pk_table-name contains a table name and fk_table-name is an empty string, the ibm_db.foreign_keys() function returns a result set that contains the primary key of the specified table and all of the foreign keys (in other tables) that refer to it.

If fk_table-name contains a table name and pk_table-name is an empty string, the ibm_db.foreign_keys() function returns a result set that contains all of the foreign keys in the specified table and the primary keys (in other tables) to which they refer.

If both pk_table-name and fk_table-name contain table names, the ibm_ db.foreign_keys() function returns the foreign keys in the table that is specified in fk_table-name, which refer to the primary key of the table that is specified in pk_table- name. There should be one key at the most.

Example

```
import ibm_db

dbstring = "DATABASE=dbname;HOSTNAME=host;PORT=port;PROTOCOL=TCPIP;UID=user
name;PWD=password"
conn = ibm_db.connect(dbstring, '', '', '')
```

```
tkey = "create table test_key(name VARCHAR(30) NOT NULL, idf INTEGER NOT
NULL)"
try:
    result = ibm_db.exec_immediate(conn, tkey)
except:
    pass

fktable = "create table foreign_key(namef VARCHAR(30) NOT NULL, id INTEGER
NOT NULL, FOREIGN KEY(namef) REFERENCES test_keys(name))"
try:
    result = ibm_db.exec_immediate(conn, fktable)
except:
    pass

stmt = ibm_db.foreign_keys(conn, None, None, None, None, None,'FOREIGN_KEY')
row = ibm_db.fetch_tuple(stmt)
print(row[7],"is a foreign key in", row[6], "referencing", row[3], "in
table", row[2])
```

If you are running this on the local Db2 system, you do not need the PROTOCOL or the
TCPIP parameter.

ibm_db.free_result

```
bool ibm_db.free_result(IBM_DBStatement stmt)
```

Description

Frees the system and IBM_DBConnections that are associated with a result set. These
resources are freed implicitly when a script finishes, but you can call ibm_db.free_
result() to explicitly free the result set resources before the end of the script. This is
really only useful for very large result sets.

This function has only one required parameter, which is an SQL stmt.

It returns True on success and False if not.

Example

```
import ibm_db

dbstring = "DATABASE=dbname;HOSTNAME=host;PORT=port;PROTOCOL=TCPIP;UID=user
name;PWD=password"
conn = ibm_db.connect(dbstring, '', '', '')

result = ibm_db.exec_immediate(conn, "select * from tabmany")
row = ibm_db.fetch_both(result)
while row:
    print(row)
    row = ibm_db.fetch_both(result)

ibm_db.free_result(result)
```

If you are running this on the local Db2 system, you do not need the PROTOCOL or the TCPIP parameter.

ibm_db.free_stmt

```
bool ibm_db.free_stmt(IBM_DBStatement stmt)
```
(DEPRECATED)

Description

Frees the system and IBM_DBConnections that are associated with a statement resource. These resources are freed implicitly when a script finishes, but you can call ibm_db.free_stmt() to explicitly free the statement resources before the end of the script.

This API is deprecated. Applications should use ibm_db.free_result() instead.

ibm_db.get_option

```
mixed ibm_db.get_option(mixed resc, int options, int type)
```

Description

Returns a value that is the current setting of a connection or statement attribute.

This function requires three parameters. The first is either an IBM_DBConnection or an IBM_DBStatement. The second parameter is a list of the options to be retrieved. The third is a type that is either 0 to indicate an IBM_DBStatement was passed as the first parameter or 1 that indicates an IBM_DBConnection was passed.

You may refer to the ibm_db.connect() for the list of options that can be set at connection and statement levels.

The function returns the current setting of the resource indicated.

Example

```
import ibm_db

# Connection options
conn_options = { ibm_db.SQL_ATTR_INFO_PROGRAMNAME : 'TestProgram'}
dbstring = "DATABASE=dbname;HOSTNAME=host;PORT=port;PROTOCOL=TCPIP;UID=user
name;PWD=password"
conn = ibm_db.connect(dbstring, '', '', conn_options)

value=ibm_db.get_option(conn, ibm_db.SQL_ATTR_INFO_PROGRAMNAME, 1)
print("Connection options:\nSQL_ATTR_INFO_PROGRAMNAME = {}".format(value),
end="\n")
returncode=ibm_db.set_option(conn, {ibm_db.SQL_ATTR_AUTOCOMMIT:0},1)
value=ibm_db.get_option(conn, ibm_db.SQL_ATTR_AUTOCOMMIT, 1)
print("SQL_ATTR_AUTOCOMMIT = {}".format(str(value)), end="\n")

# statement options
stmt = ibm_db.prepare(conn, "select * from tabmany")
returnCode = ibm_db.set_option(stmt, {ibm_db.SQL_ATTR_QUERY_TIMEOUT : 20}, 0)
value = ibm_db.get_option(stmt, ibm_db.SQL_ATTR_QUERY_TIMEOUT, 0)
print("Statement options:\nSQL_ATTR_QUERY_TIMEOUT = {}".format(str(value)),
end="\n")
result = ibm_db.execute(stmt)
```

```
if result:
    ibm_db.free_result(stmt)
else:
    print(ibm_db..stmt_errormsg())
ibm_db.rollback(conn)
ibm_db.close(conn)
```

If you are running this on the local Db2 system, you do not need the PROTOCOL or the TCPIP parameter.

ibm_db.next_result

```
IBM_DBStatement ibm_db.next_result(IBM_DBStatement stmt)
```

Description

Requests the next result set from a stored procedure. A stored procedure can return zero or more result sets. While you handle the first result set in exactly the same way you would handle the results returned by a simple SELECT statement, to fetch the second and subsequent result sets from a stored procedure, you must call the ibm_db.next_result() function and return the result to a uniquely named Python variable.

This function has one required parameter, which is an SQL stmt.

It returns a new IBM_DBStatement containing the next result set or False if no result set is available.

Example

```
import ibm_db

dbstring = "DATABASE=dbname;HOSTNAME=host;PORT=port;PROTOCOL=TCPIP;UID=user
name;PWD=password"
conn = ibm_db.connect(dbstring, '', '', '')

create_proc = """create procedure multi_results()
result sets 3
language sql
Begin
DECLARE c1 CURSOR WITH RETURN FOR
select name, id from tabmany;
```

```python
DECLARE c2 CURSOR WITH RETURN FOR
select name, id from tabmany where id < 40;

DECLARE c3 CURSOR WITH RETURN FOR
select name, id from tabmany where id > 40;

OPEN c1;
OPEN c2;
OPEN c3;
END """

try:
    rc = ibm_db.exec_immediate(conn, create_proc)
except:
    pass

# retrieve first result set
resultSet_1 = None
try:
    resultSet_1 = ibm_db.callproc(conn, 'multi_results')
except:
    print("stored procedure invocation\n")
    print(ibm_db.stmt_errormsg())
    pass

if resultSet_1:
    row = ibm_db.fetch_tuple(resultSet_1)
    while row:
        for i in row:
            print(i)
        row = ibm_db.fetch_tuple(resultSet_1)

# retrieve second result set
resultSet_2 = None
try:
    resultSet_2 = ibm_db.next_result(resultSet_1)
except Exception:
    pass
```

```
if resultSet_2:
    row = ibm_db.fetch_tuple(resultSet_2)
    while row:
        for i in row:
            print(i)
        row = ibm_db.fetch_tuple(resultSet_2)

# retrieve third result set
resultSet_3 = None
try:
    resultSet_3 = ibm_db.next_result(resultSet_1)
except Exception:
    pass

if resultSet_3:
    row = ibm_db.fetch_tuple(resultSet_3)
    while row:
        for i in row:
            print(i)
        row = ibm_db.fetch_tuple(resultSet_3)
```

If you are running this on the local Db2 system, you do not need the PROTOCOL or the TCPIP parameter.

ibm_db.num_fields

```
int ibm_db.num_fields(IBM_DBStatement stmt)
```

Description

Returns the number of fields contained in a result set. This is most useful for handling result sets returned by dynamically generated queries or for result sets returned by stored procedures, where your application cannot otherwise know how to retrieve and use the results.

This function has only one required parameter, which is an SQL stmt.

It returns the number of fields in the result set specified by the SQL stmt. It returns False if there was an error.

Example

```
import ibm_db

dbstring = "DATABASE=dbname;HOSTNAME=host;PORT=port;PROTOCOL=TCPIP;UID=user
name;PWD=password"
conn = ibm_db.connect(dbstring, '', '', '')

sql = "select id, name from tabmany"
stmt = ibm_db.prepare(conn, sql,)
result = ibm_db.execute(stmt)
cols = ibm_db.num_fields(stmt)
print(cols)
```

If you are running this on the local Db2 system, you do not need the PROTOCOL or the TCPIP parameter.

ibm_db.num_rows

```
int ibm_db.num_rows(IBM_DBStatement stmt)
```

Description

Returns the number of rows deleted, inserted, or updated by an SQL statement.

To determine the number of rows that will be returned by a SELECT statement, issue SELECT COUNT(*) with the same predicates as your intended SELECT statement and retrieve the value. If your application logic checks the number of rows returned by a SELECT statement and branches if the number of rows is 0, consider modifying your application to attempt to return the first row with one of ibm_db.fetch_assoc(), ibm_db.fetch_both(), ibm_db.fetch_tuple(), or ibm_db.fetch_row(), and branch if the fetch function returns False.

This function has one required parameter, which is an SQL stmt.

It returns the number of rows affected by the stmt handle.

> **Note**   If you issue a SELECT statement using a scrollable cursor, ibm_db.num_
> rows() returns the number of rows returned by the SELECT statement. However,
> the overhead associated with scrollable cursors significantly degrades the
> performance of your application, so if this is the only reason you are considering
> using scrollable cursors, you should use a forward-only cursor and either call
> SELECT COUNT(*) or rely on the Boolean return value of the fetch functions to
> achieve the equivalent functionality with much better performance.

Example

```
import ibm_db

dbstring = "DATABASE=dbname;HOSTNAME=host;PORT=port;PROTOCOL=TCPIP;UID=user
name;PWD=password"
conn = ibm_db.connect(dbstring, '', '', '')

sql = "update tabmany set id=15 where id < 40"
res = ibm_db.exec_immediate(conn, sql)
print ("Number of affected rows: %d" % ibm_db.num_rows(res))
ibm_db.rollback(conn)
ibm_db.close(conn)
```

If you are running this on the local Db2 system, you do not need the PROTOCOL or the
TCPIP parameter.

ibm_db.pconnect

```
IBM_DBStatement ibm_db.pconnect(string database, string username, string
password [, dict options])
```

Description

Returns a persistent connection to an IBM Db2 Universal Database, IBM Cloudscape,
Apache Derby, or Informix. Persistent connections are not closed when ibm_db.close()
is called on them. Instead, they are returned to a process-wide connection pool.

The next time `ibm_db.pconnect()` is called, the connection pool is searched for a matching connection. If one is found, it is returned to the application instead of attempting a new connection.

For more information on parameters and return values, see `ibm_db.connect()`.

Example

```
import ibm_db

# Open normal connection
dbstring = "DATABASE=dbname;HOSTNAME=host;PORT=port;PROTOCOL=TCPIP;UID=user
name;PWD=password"
conn = ibm_db.connect(dbstring, '', '', '')
print("Normal connection 1 = {}".format(conn1))
# Open persistent connections
pconn1 = ibm_db.pconnect('DATABASE=database;HOSTNAME=hostname;PORT=port;PRO
TOCOL=TCPIP;UID=username;PWD=password','','')
print("Persistent connection 1 = {}".format(pconn1))
# pconn2 is same as pconn1
pconn2 = ibm_db.pconnect('DATABASE=database;HOSTNAME=hostname;PORT=port;PRO
TOCOL=TCPIP;UID=username;PWD=password','','')
print("Persistent connection 2 = {}".format(pconn2))

# closing normal connection
ibm_db.close(conn1)
print("Normal connection 1 = {} closed".format(conn1))
# closing persistent connection will not shut off the db connection
ibm_db.close(pconn1)
print("Persistent connection 1 = {} closed".format(pconn1))

# select from the persistent connection
sql = "select * from tabmany"
stmt = ibm_db.exec_immediate(pconn2,sql)

# fetching data from a closed connection results in error
try:
    sql = "select * from tabmany"
    stmt = ibm_db.exec_immediate(conn1,sql)
```

```
except:
    print("Connection is closed, Hence can't execute {} on conn1".
    format(sql))
    pass
```

If you are running this on the local Db2 system, you do not need the PROTOCOL or the TCPIP parameter.

ibm_db.prepare

```
IBMDB_Statement ibm_db.prepare(IBM_DBConnection connection, string
statement [, dict options])
```

Description

Creates a prepared SQL statement that can include zero or more parameter markers (? characters) representing parameters for input, output, or input/output. You can pass parameters to the prepared statement using ibm_db.bind_param(), or for input values only, a tuple is passed to ibm_db.execute().

This function has two required parameters and one optional parameter.

Parameters

- connection: A valid IBM_DBConnection

- statement: An SQL statement, optionally containing one or more parameter markers.

- options (optional): A dict containing statement options:

  - SQL_ATTR_CURSOR_TYPE: Set the cursor type to one of the following (not supported on all databases):

    - SQL_CURSOR_FORWARD_ONLY

    - SQL_CURSOR_KEYSET_DRIVEN

    - SQL_CURSOR_DYNAMIC

    - SQL_CURSOR_STATIC

Return Values

Returns an IBM_DBStatement object if the SQL statement was successfully parsed and prepared by the database server or False if the database server returned an error.

Example

```
import ibm_db

dbstring = "DATABASE=dbname;HOSTNAME=host;PORT=port;PROTOCOL=TCPIP;UID=user
name;PWD=password"
conn = ibm_db.connect(dbstring, '', '', '')

stmt=ibm_db.prepare(conn, "select * from tabmany where id=?", {ibm_db.SQL_
ATTR_CURSOR_TYPE: ibm_db.SQL_CURSOR_STATIC})
id=1
ibm_db.bind_param(stmt, 1,id)
ibm_db.execute(stmt)
row=ibm_db.fetch_tuple(stmt)
print(row)
```

If you are running this on the local Db2 system, you do not need the PROTOCOL or the TCPIP parameter.

ibm_db.primary_keys

```
IBM_DBStatement ibm_db.primary_keys(IBM_DBConnection connection, string
qualifier, string schema, string table-name)
```

Description

Returns a result set listing the primary keys for a table.

This function has four required parameters. The first is a valid IBM_DBConnection. The second is a qualifier that is only used in the mainframe environment. The third is the schema that contains the tables or None for the current schema. The fourth is the name of the table.

Return Values

Returns an IBM_DBStatement with a result set containing the following columns:

- TABLE_CAT: Name of the catalog for the table containing the primary key. The value is None if this table does not have catalogs.

- TABLE_SCHEM: Name of the schema for the table containing the primary key.

- TABLE_NAME: Name of the table containing the primary key.

- COLUMN_NAME: Name of the column containing the primary key.

- KEY_SEQ: 1-indexed position of the column in the key.

- PK_NAME: The name of the primary key.

Example

```
import ibm_db

dbstring = "DATABASE=dbname;HOSTNAME=host;PORT=port;PROTOCOL=TCPIP;UID=user
name;PWD=password"
conn = ibm_db.connect(dbstring, '', '', '')

stmt = ibm_db.exec_immediate(conn,"drop table test_primary_keys")
statement = 'CREATE TABLE test_primary_keys (id INTEGER NOT NULL, PRIMARY
KEY(id))'
result = ibm_db.exec_immediate(conn, statement)
stmt = ibm_db.primary_keys(conn, None, None, 'TEST_PRIMARY_KEYS')
row = ibm_db.fetch_tuple(stmt)
print("{} is primary key in table {} with index position {} in the key".
format(row[3],row[2],row[4]))
```

If you are running this on the local Db2 system, you do not need the PROTOCOL or the TCPIP parameter.

ibm_db.procedure_columns

IBM_DBStatement ibm_db.procedure_columns(IBM_DBConnection connection, string qualifier, string schema, string procedure, string parameter)

Description

Returns a result set listing the parameters for one or more stored procedures.

This function has five required parameters. The first is a valid IBM_DBConnection. The second is a qualifier that is only used in the mainframe environment. The third is the schema that contains the procedure. The fourth is the name of the procedure. The fifth is the name of the parameter or *None*.

Return Values

Returns an IBM_DBStatement with a result set containing the following columns:

- PROCEDURE_CAT: The catalog that contains the procedure. The value is None if this table does not have catalogs.

- PROCEDURE_SCHEM: Name of the schema that contains the stored procedure.

- PROCEDURE_NAME: Name of the procedure.

- COLUMN_NAME: Name of the parameter.

- COLUMN_TYPE: An integer value representing the type of the parameter:

    - 1 (SQL_PARAM_INPUT): Input (IN) parameter

    - 2 (SQL_PARAM_INPUT_OUTPUT): Input/output (INOUT) parameter

    - 3 (SQL_PARAM_OUTPUT): Output (OUT) parameter

- DATA_TYPE: An integer value indicating the SQL data type for the parameter.

- TYPE_NAME: A string representing the data type for the parameter.

- COLUMN_SIZE: An integer value representing the size of the parameter.

- BUFFER_LENGTH: Maximum number of bytes necessary to store data for this parameter.

- DECIMAL_DIGITS: The scale of the parameter, or None where scale is not applicable.

- NUM_PREC_RADIX: An integer value of either 10 (representing an exact numeric data type), 2 (representing an approximate numeric data type), or None (representing a data type for which radix is not applicable).

- NULLABLE: An integer value representing whether the parameter is nullable or not.

- REMARKS: Description of the parameter.

- COLUMN_DEF: Default value for the parameter.

- SQL_DATA_TYPE: An integer value representing the size of the parameter.

- SQL_DATETIME_SUB: Returns an integer value representing a datetime subtype code, or None for SQL data types to which this does not apply.

- CHAR_OCTET_LENGTH: Maximum length in octets for a character data type parameter, which matches COLUMN_SIZE for single-byte character set data or None for non-character data types.

- ORDINAL_POSITION: The 1-indexed position of the parameter in the CALL statement.

- IS_NULLABLE: A string value where 'YES' means that the parameter accepts or returns None values and 'NO' means that the parameter does not accept or return None values.

Example

```
import ibm_db

dbstring = "DATABASE=dbname;HOSTNAME=host;PORT=port;PROTOCOL=TCPIP;UID=user
name;PWD=password"
conn = ibm_db.connect(dbstring, '', '', '')

sql="""create or replace procedure proc(OUT out1 integer) dynamic result
sets 1 begin  select id into out1 from tabmany where id=1; end"""
ibm_db.exec_immediate(conn, sql)
# note the procedure name upper case
resultSet = ibm_db.procedure_columns(conn, None, '', 'PROC', None)
#print(resultSet)
row = ibm_db.fetch_assoc(resultSet)
while row:
    print(row)
    print("Procedure {} is having one output parameter with name {}\n".
    format(row['PROCEDURE_NAME'], row['COLUMN_NAME']))
    row = ibm_db.fetch_assoc(resultSet)
```

If you are running this on the local Db2 system, you do not need the PROTOCOL or the TCPIP parameter.

ibm_db.procedures

```
resource ibm_db.procedures(IBM_DBConnection connection, string qualifier,
string schema, string procedure)
```

Description

Returns a result set listing the stored procedures registered in a database.

This function has four required parameters. The first is an IBM_DBConnection connection. The second is a string qualifier only needed for mainframe databases. The third parameter is the database schema. The fourth and last parameter is the name of the procedure that can contain the _ (underscore) and % wildcards.

Return Values

Returns an IBM_DBStatement with a result set containing the following columns:

- PROCEDURE_CAT: The catalog that contains the procedure. The value is None if this table does not have catalogs.

- PROCEDURE_SCHEM: Name of the schema that contains the stored procedure.

- PROCEDURE_NAME: Name of the procedure.

- NUM_INPUT_PARAMS: Number of input (IN) parameters for the stored procedure.

- NUM_OUTPUT_PARAMS: Number of output (OUT) parameters for the stored procedure.

- NUM_RESULT_SETS: Number of result sets returned by the stored procedure.

- REMARKS: Any comments about the stored procedure.

- PROCEDURE_TYPE: Always returns 1, indicating that the stored procedure does not return a return value.

Example

```
import ibm_db

dbstring = "DATABASE=dbname;HOSTNAME=host;PORT=port;PROTOCOL=TCPIP;UID=user
name;PWD=password"
conn = ibm_db.connect(dbstring, '', '', '')

schemaName = 'DB2ADMIN'
resultSet = ibm_db.procedures(conn, None, schemaName, 'PROC')
row = ibm_db.fetch_assoc(resultSet)
while row:
    print(row)
    row = ibm_db.fetch_assoc(resultSet)
```

If you are running this on the local Db2 system, you do not need the PROTOCOL or the TCPIP parameter.

ibm_db.recreatedb

```
bool ibm_db.recreatedb(IBM_DBConnection connection, string dbName
[, codeSet, mode])
```

Description

Drops and then recreates a database by using the specified database name, code set, and mode.

This function has two required and two optional parameters. The first parameter is an IBM_DBConnection connection. The second parameter is the database name dbName. The third parameter is optional and is the codeSet of the database. The fourth parameter is optional and is the mode for the database.

The function returns True if the database is created successfully or None if there was an error.

Example

```
import ibm_db
conn_str_attach = "attach=true;HOSTNAME=hostname;PORT=port;PROTOCOL=TCPIP;
UID=username;PWD=password"
database='test123'
conn_attach = ibm_db.connect(conn_str_attach, '', '')

rc = ibm_db.recreatedb(conn_attach, database)
```

If you are running this on the local Db2 system, you do not need the PROTOCOL or the TCPIP parameter.

ibm_db.result

```
mixed ibm_db.result(IBM_DBStatement stmt, mixed column)
```

Description

Returns a single column from a row in the result set. Use ibm_db.result() to return the value of a specified column in the current row of a result set. You must call ibm_db.fetch_row() before calling ibm_db.result() to set the location of the result set pointer.

This function has two required parameters. The first is an IBM_DBStatement stmt. The second is the column to return, which can be a 0-indexed column or the name of the column.

The function returns the contents of the specified column or None in the case of an error.

Example

```
import ibm_db
conn=ibm_db.connect("DATABASE=database;HOSTNAME=hostname;PORT=port;PROTOCOL
=TCPIP;UID=username;PWD=password",'','')

sql = "select id, name from tabmany"
stmt = ibm_db.exec_immediate(conn, sql)
while (ibm_db.fetch_row(stmt)):
    id = ibm_db.result(stmt, "ID")
    name = ibm_db.result(stmt, "NAME")
    print("col1 = {}, col2 = {}".format(id, name))
```

If you are running this on the local Db2 system, you do not need the PROTOCOL or the TCPIP parameter.

ibm_db.rollback

```
bool ibm_db.rollback(IBM_DBConnection connection)
```

Description

Rolls back an in-progress transaction on the specified IBM_DBConnection and begins a new transaction. Python applications normally default to AUTOCOMMIT mode, so ibm_db.rollback() normally has no effect unless AUTOCOMMIT has been turned off for the IBM_DBConnection. Note: If the specified IBM_DBConnection is a persistent connection, all transactions in progress for all applications using that persistent connection will be rolled back. For this reason, persistent connections are not recommended for use in applications that require transactions.

This function has only one required parameter, which is an IBM_DBConnection connection.

It returns True on success or False on an error.

Example

```
import ibm_db

dbstring = "DATABASE=dbname;HOSTNAME=host;PORT=port;PROTOCOL=TCPIP;UID=user
name;PWD=password"
conn = ibm_db.connect(dbstring, '', '', ,{ibm_db.SQL_ATTR_AUTOCOMMIT:
bm_db.SQL_AUTOCOMMIT_OFF})

sql = "insert into tabmany values(100, 'Testrollback')"
stmt = ibm_db.exec_immediate(conn, sql)
sql = "select name from tabmany where id=100"
stmt = ibm_db.exec_immediate(conn, sql)
res = ibm_db.fetch_tuple(stmt)
print(res)

# rollback
rc = ibm_db.rollback(conn)

# again fetch the data, should see empty row
stmt1 = ibm_db.exec_immediate(conn, sql)
res1 = ibm_db.fetch_tuple(stmt1)
print(res1)
```

If you are running this on the local Db2 system, you do not need the PROTOCOL or the TCPIP parameter.

bm_db.server_info

```
IBM_DBServerInfo ibm_db.server_info ( IBM_DBConnection connection )
```

Description

Returns a read-only object with information about the IBM Db2 or Informix server.

This function has only one required parameter, which is an IBM_DBConnection connection.

Return Values

On success, an object has the following fields:

- DBMS_NAME: The name of the database server to which you are connected. For Db2 servers, this is a combination of Db2 followed by the operating system on which the database server is running (string).

- DBMS_VER: The version of the database server, in the form of a string "MM.mm.uuuu" where MM is the major version, mm is the minor version, and uuuu is the update. For example, "08.02.0001" represents major version 8, minor version 2, and update 1 (string).

- DB_CODEPAGE: The code page of the database to which you are connected (int).

- DB_NAME: The name of the database to which you are connected (string).

- DFT_ISOLATION: The default transaction isolation level supported by the server (string).

- UR (uncommitted read): Changes are immediately visible by all concurrent transactions.

- CS (cursor stability): A row read by one transaction can be altered and committed by a second concurrent transaction.

- RS (read stability): A transaction can add or remove rows matching a search condition or a pending transaction.

- RR (repeatable read): Data affected by a pending transaction is not available to other transactions.

- NC (no commit): Any changes are visible at the end of a successful operation. Explicit commits and rollbacks are not allowed.

- IDENTIFIER_QUOTE_CHAR: The character used to delimit an identifier (string).

- INST_NAME: The instance on the database server that contains the database (string).

- ISOLATION_OPTION: A tuple of the isolation options supported by the database server. The isolation options are described in the DFT_ISOLATION property (tuple).

- KEYWORDS: A tuple of the keywords reserved by the database server (tuple).

- LIKE_ESCAPE_CLAUSE: True if the database server supports the use of % and _wildcard characters. False if the database server does not support these wildcard characters (bool).

- MAX_COL_NAME_LEN: Maximum length of a column name supported by the database server, expressed in bytes (int).

- MAX_IDENTIFIER_LEN: Maximum length of an SQL identifier supported by the database server, expressed in characters (int).

- MAX_INDEX_SIZE: Maximum size of columns combined in an index supported by the database server, expressed in bytes (int).

- MAX_PROC_NAME_LEN: Maximum length of a procedure name supported by the database server, expressed in bytes (int).

- MAX_ROW_SIZE: Maximum length of a row in a base table supported by the database server, expressed in bytes (int).

- MAX_SCHEMA_NAME_LEN: Maximum length of a schema name supported by the database server, expressed in bytes (int).

- MAX_STATEMENT_LEN: Maximum length of an SQL statement supported by the database server, expressed in bytes (int).

- MAX_TABLE_NAME_LEN: Maximum length of a table name supported by the database server, expressed in bytes (bool).

- NON_NULLABLE_COLUMNS: True if the database server supports columns that can be defined as NOT NULL and False if the database server does not support columns defined as NOT NULL (bool).

- PROCEDURES: True if the database server supports the use of the CALL statement to call stored procedures and False if the database server does not support the CALL statement (bool).

- SPECIAL_CHARS: A string containing all of the characters other than A–Z, 0–9, and underscore that can be used in an identifier name (string).

- SQL_CONFORMANCE: The level of conformance to the ANSI/ISO SQL-92 specification offered by the database server (string).

- ENTRY: Entry-level SQL-92 compliance.

- FIPS127: FIPS-127-2 transitional compliance.

- FULL: Full-level SQL-92 compliance.

- INTERMEDIATE: Intermediate-level SQL-92 compliance.

On failure, returns `False`.

Example

```
import ibm_db

dbstring = "DATABASE=dbname;HOSTNAME=host;PORT=port;PROTOCOL=TCPIP;UID=user
name;PWD=password"
conn = ibm_db.connect(dbstring, '', '', '')

serverInfo = ibm_db.server_info(conn)
print("Db2 database server name                : {}" .format(serverInfo.
                                                  DBMS_NAME))

print("Database name                           : {}" .format(serverInfo.
                                                  DB_NAME))

print("Db2 instance name                       : {}" .format(serverInfo.
                                                  INST_NAME))

print("Database codepage used                  : {}" .format(serverInfo.
                                                  DB_CODEPAGE))
```

If you are running this on the local Db2 system, you do not need the PROTOCOL or the TCPIP parameter.

ibm_db.set_option

```
bool ibm_db.set_option(mixed resc, dict options, int type)
```

Description

Sets options for an IBM_DBConnection or IBM_DBStatement. You cannot set options for result set resources.

This function has three required parameters. The first is a valid IBM_DBConnection resc or an IBM_DBStatement resc. The second is a Python dict containing the option and its new value. The third parameter is either 0 for an IBM_DBStatement or 1 for an IBM_DBConnection.

The function returns True on success or False if there was an error.

Example

```
import ibm_db

conn_options = { ibm_db.SQL_ATTR_INFO_PROGRAMNAME : 'TestProgram'}
dbstring = "DATABASE=dbname;HOSTNAME=host;PORT=port;PROTOCOL=TCPIP;UID=user
name;PWD=password"
conn = ibm_db.connect(dbstring, '', '', conn_options)

value = ibm_db.get_option(conn, ibm_db.SQL_ATTR_INFO_PROGRAMNAME, 1)
print("Connection options:\nSQL_ATTR_INFO_PROGRAMNAME = {}".format(value),
end="\n")
returncode = ibm_db.set_option(conn, {ibm_db.SQL_ATTR_AUTOCOMMIT:0},1)
value = ibm_db.get_option(conn, ibm_db.SQL_ATTR_AUTOCOMMIT, 1)
print("SQL_ATTR_AUTOCOMMIT = {}".format(str(value)), end="\n")

# statement options
stmt = ibm_db.prepare(conn, "select * from tabmany")
returnCode = ibm_db.set_option(stmt, {ibm_db.SQL_ATTR_QUERY_TIMEOUT : 20}, 0)
value = ibm_db.get_option(stmt, ibm_db.SQL_ATTR_QUERY_TIMEOUT, 0)
print("Statement options:\nSQL_ATTR_QUERY_TIMEOUT = {}".format(str(value)),
end="\n")
result = ibm_db.execute(stmt)

if result:
    ibm_db.free_result(stmt)
```

```
else:
    print(ibm_db..stmt_errormsg())
ibm_db.rollback(conn)
ibm_db.close(conn)
```

If you are running this on the local Db2 system, you do not need the PROTOCOL or the TCPIP parameter.

ibm_db.special_columns

IBM_DBStatement ibm_db.special_columns(IBM_DBConnection connection, string qualifier, string schema, string table_name, int scope)

Description

Returns a result set listing the unique row identifier columns for a table.

This function has a number of parameters. See the following for a complete list.

Parameters

- Connection: A valid IBM_DBConnection.

- Qualifier: A qualifier for Db2 databases running on OS/390 or z/OS servers. For other databases, pass None or an empty string.

- schema: The schema that contains the tables.

- table_name: The name of the table.

- scope: Integer value representing the minimum duration for which the unique row identifier is valid. This can be one of the following values:

  - 0: Row identifier is valid only while the cursor is positioned on the row (SQL_SCOPE_CURROW).

  - 1: Row identifier is valid for the duration of the transaction (SQL_SCOPE_TRANSACTION).

  - 2: Row identifier is valid for the duration of the connection (SQL_SCOPE_SESSION).

Return Values

Returns an IBM_DBStatement with a result set containing the following columns:

SCOPE: Integer value representing the minimum duration for which the unique row identifier is valid:

- 0 (SQL_SCOPE_CURROW): Row identifier is valid only while the cursor is positioned on the row.

- 1 (SQL_SCOPE_TRANSACTION): Row identifier is valid for the duration of the transaction.

- 2 (SQL_SCOPE_SESSION): Row identifier is valid for the duration of the connection.

COLUMN_NAME: Name of the unique column

DATA_TYPE: SQL data type for the column

TYPE_NAME: Character string representation of the SQL data type for the column

COLUMN_SIZE: An integer value representing the size of the column

BUFFER_LENGTH: Maximum number of bytes necessary to store data from this column

DECIMAL_DIGITS: The scale of the column, or None where scale is not applicable

NUM_PREC_RADIX: An integer value of either 10 (representing an exact numeric data type), 2 (representing an approximate numeric data type), or None (representing a data type for which radix is not applicable).

PSEUDO_COLUMN: Always returns 1

Example

```
import ibm_db

dbstring = "DATABASE=dbname;HOSTNAME=host;PORT=port;PROTOCOL=TCPIP;UID=user
name;PWD=password"
conn = ibm_db.connect(dbstring, '', '', '')

schemaName = "DB2ADMIN"
tableName = "TABMANY"
resultSet = ibm_db.special_columns(conn, None, schemaName, tableName, 0)
dataRecord = ibm_db.fetch_assoc(resultSet)
```

```
while dataRecord:
    print("Column name              : {}" .format(dataRecord['COLUMN_NAME']))
    print("Data type                : {}" .format(dataRecord['TYPE_NAME']))
    print("Column size              : {}" .format(dataRecord['COLUMN_SIZE']))
```

If you are running this on the local Db2 system, you do not need the PROTOCOL or the TCPIP parameter.

ibm_db.statistics

```
IBM_DBStatement ibm_db.statistics(IBM_DBConnection connection, string
qualifier, string schema, string table-name, bool unique)
```

Description

Returns a result set listing the index and statistics for a table.

This function has a number of required parameters. The first is a valid IBM_DBConnection connection. The second is a qualifier that is only used for a mainframe database. The third is the schema name for the table. The fourth is the table name of the table. And the fifth is a bool value containing False for only the information of the index information or True for all table indexes.

Return Values

Returns an IBM_DBStatement with a result set containing the following columns:

TABLE_CAT: The catalog that contains the table. The value is None if this table does not have catalogs.

TABLE_SCHEM: Name of the schema that contains the table.

TABLE_NAME: Name of the table.

NON_UNIQUE: An integer value representing whether the index prohibits unique values or whether the row represents statistics on the table itself:

- 0 (SQL_FALSE): The index allows duplicate values.

- 1 (SQL_TRUE): The index values must be unique.

- None: This row is statistics information for the table itself.

INDEX_QUALIFIER: A string value representing the qualifier that would have to be prepended to INDEX_NAME to fully qualify the index.

INDEX_NAME: A string representing the name of the index.

TYPE: An integer value representing the type of information contained in this row of the result set:

- 0 (SQL_TABLE_STAT): The row contains statistics about the table itself.

- 1 (SQL_INDEX_CLUSTERED): The row contains information about a clustered index.

- 2 (SQL_INDEX_HASH): The row contains information about a hashed index.

- 3 (SQL_INDEX_OTHER): The row contains information about a type of index that is neither clustered nor hashed.

ORDINAL_POSITION: The 1-indexed position of the column in the index. None if the row contains statistics information about the table itself.

COLUMN_NAME: The name of the column in the index. None if the row contains statistics information about the table itself.

ASC_OR_DESC: A if the column is sorted in ascending order, D if the column is sorted in descending order, and None if the row contains statistics information about the table itself.

CARDINALITY: If the row contains information about an index, this column contains an integer value representing the number of unique values in the index. If the row contains information about the table itself, this column contains an integer value representing the number of rows in the table.

PAGES: If the row contains information about an index, this column contains an integer value representing the number of pages used to store the index. If the row contains information about the table itself, this column contains an integer value representing the number of pages used to store the table.

FILTER_CONDITION: Always returns None.

Example

```
import ibm_db

dbstring = "DATABASE=dbname;HOSTNAME=host;PORT=port;PROTOCOL=TCPIP;UID=user
name;PWD=password"
conn = ibm_db.connect(dbstring, '', '', '')

create_table = "create table index_test(id int, data VARCHAR(50))"
rc = ibm_db.exec_immediate(conn, create_table)
create_index = "CREATE UNIQUE INDEX index1 ON index_test (id)"
rc = ibm_db.exec_immediate(conn, create_index)

schemaName = "DB2ADMIN"
tableName = "INDEX_TEST"
resultSet = ibm_db.statistics(conn, None, schemaName, tableName, True)
dataRecord = ibm_db.fetch_assoc(resultSet)
while dataRecord['INDEX_NAME'] is not None:
    print("Table Schema                       : {}" .format(dataRecord
                                                    ['TABLE_SCHEM']))
    print("Table name                         : {}" .format(dataRecord
                                                    ['TABLE_NAME']))
    print("Index qualifier                    : {}" .format(dataRecord
                                                    ['INDEX_QUALIFIER']))
    print("Index name                         : {}" .format(dataRecord
                                                    ['INDEX_NAME']))
    print("Column name                        : {}" .format(dataRecord
                                                    ['COLUMN_NAME']))
    print("Column position in index           : {}" .format(dataRecord
                                                    ['ORDINAL_POSITION']))
```

If you are running this on the local Db2 system, you do not need the PROTOCOL or the TCPIP parameter.

```
    dataRecord = ibm_db.fetch_assoc(resultSet)
```

ibm_db.stmt_error

```
string ibm_db.stmt_error([IBM_DBStatement stmt])
```

Description

When no parameters are passed, returns the SQLSTATE representing the reason the last attempt to return an IBM_DBStatement via ibm_db.prepare(), ibm_db.exec_immediate(), or ibm_db.callproc() failed.

When passed a valid IBM_DBStatement, returns the SQLSTATE representing the reason the last operation using the resource failed.

This function has only one optional parameter, which is a valid IBM_DBStatement stmt.

The return value for the function will contain the SQLSTATE value or an empty string if there was no error.

Example

```
import ibm_db

dbstring = "DATABASE=dbname;HOSTNAME=host;PORT=port;PROTOCOL=TCPIP;UID=user name;PWD=password"
conn = ibm_db.connect(dbstring, '', '', '')

create_table = "create table index_test(id int, data VARCHAR(50)"
try:
    rc = ibm_db.exec_immediate(conn, create_table)
except:
    print("Query ' {} ' failed with ".format(create_table))
    print("SQLSTATE = {}".format(ibm_db.stmt_error()))
```

If you are running this on the local Db2 system, you do not need the PROTOCOL or the TCPIP parameter.

ibm_db.stmt_errormsg

```
string ibm_db.stmt_errormsg([IBM_DBStatement stmt])
```

Description

When no parameters are passed, returns a string containing the SQLCODE and error message representing the reason the last attempt to return an IBM_DBStatement via ibm_db.prepare(), ibm_db.exec_immediate(), or ibm_db.callproc() failed.

When passed a valid IBM_DBStatement, returns a string containing the SQLCODE and error message representing the reason the last operation using the resource failed.

Example

```
import ibm_db

dbstring = "DATABASE=dbname;HOSTNAME=host;PORT=port;PROTOCOL=TCPIP;UID=user
name;PWD=password"
conn = ibm_db.connect(dbstring, '', '', '')

create_table = "create table index_test(id int, data VARCHAR(50)"
try:
    rc = ibm_db.exec_immediate(conn, create_table)
except:
    print("Query ' {} ' failed with ".format(create_table))
    print("Error : {}".format(ibm_db.stmt_errormsg()))
```

If you are running this on the local Db2 system, you do not need the PROTOCOL or the TCPIP parameter.

ibm_db.table_privileges

```
IBM_DBStatement ibm_db.table_privileges(IBM_DBConnection connection [,
string qualifier [, string schema [, string table_name]]])
```

Description

Returns a result set listing the tables and associated privileges in a database.

This function has only one required parameter, which is an IBM_DBConnection connection. The qualifier is optional and is only used by mainframe databases. The schema is optional and contains the schema for the database. The table-name is optional and restricts the information returned to a single table.

Return Values

Returns an IBM_DBStatement with a result set containing following columns:

TABLE_CAT: The catalog that contains the table. The value is None if this table does not have catalogs.

TABLE_SCHEM: Name of the schema that contains the table.

TABLE_NAME: Name of the table.

GRANTOR: Authorization ID of the user who granted the privilege.

GRANTEE: Authorization ID of the user to whom the privilege was granted.

PRIVILEGE: The privilege that has been granted. This can be one of ALTER, CONTROL, DELETE, INDEX, INSERT, REFERENCES, SELECT, or UPDATE.

IS_GRANTABLE: A string value of "YES" or "NO" indicating whether the grantee can grant the privilege to other users.

Example

```
import ibm_db

dbstring = "DATABASE=dbname;HOSTNAME=host;PORT=port;PROTOCOL=TCPIP;UID=user
name;PWD=password"
conn = ibm_db.connect(dbstring, '', '', '')

schemaName = "DB2ADMIN"
tableName = "TABMANY"
resultSet = ibm_db.table_privileges(conn, None, schemaName, tableName)
dataRecord = ibm_db.fetch_assoc(resultSet)
print("Schema name          : {}" .format(dataRecord['TABLE_SCHEM']))
print("Table name           : {}" .format(dataRecord['TABLE_NAME']))
print("Privilege grantor    : {}" .format(dataRecord['GRANTOR']))
print("Privilege recipient  : {}" .format(dataRecord['GRANTEE']))
print("Privilege            : {}" .format(dataRecord['PRIVILEGE']))
print("Privilege is grantable : {}" .format(dataRecord['IS_GRANTABLE']))
```

If you are running this on the local Db2 system, you do not need the PROTOCOL or the TCPIP parameter.

ibm_db.tables

IBM_DBStatement ibm_db.tables(IBM_DBConnection connection [, string qualifier [, string schema [, string table-name [, string table-type]]]])

Description

Returns a result set listing the tables and associated metadata in a database.

Parameters

- Connection: A valid IBM_DBConnection.

- qualifier (optional): A qualifier for Db2 databases running on OS/390 or z/OS servers. For other databases, pass None or an empty string.

- schema (optional): The schema that contains the tables. This parameter accepts a search pattern containing _ (underscore) and % as wildcards.

- table-name (optional): The name of the table. This parameter accepts a search pattern containing_ and % as wildcards.

- table-type (optional): A list of comma-delimited table type identifiers. To match all table types, pass None or an empty string.

    - ALIAS

    - HIERARCHY TABLE

    - INOPERATIVE VIEW

    - NICKNAME

    - MATERIALIZED QUERY TABLE

    - SYSTEM TABLE

    - TABLE

    - TYPED TABLE

    - TYPED VIEW

    - VIEW

Return Values

Returns an IBM_DBStatement with a result set containing the following columns:

TABLE_CAT: The catalog that contains the table. The value is None if this table does not have catalogs.

TABLE_SCHEMA: Name of the schema that contains the table.

TABLE_NAME: Name of the table.

TABLE_TYPE: Table type identifier for the table.

REMARKS: Description of the table.

Example

```
import ibm_db

dbstring = "DATABASE=dbname;HOSTNAME=host;PORT=port;PROTOCOL=TCPIP;UID=user
name;PWD=password"
conn = ibm_db.connect(dbstring, '', '', '')

schemaName = "DB2ADMIN"
resultSet = ibm_db.tables(conn, None, schemaName, 'TAB%', 'TABLE')
dataRecord = ibm_db.fetch_assoc(resultSet)
while dataRecord:
    print("Table schema  : {}" .format(dataRecord['TABLE_SCHEM']))
    print("Table name    : {}" .format(dataRecord['TABLE_NAME']))
    print("Table type    : {}" .format(dataRecord['TABLE_TYPE']))
    print("Description   : {}" .format(dataRecord['REMARKS']))
    dataRecord = ibm_db.fetch_assoc(resultSet)
    print("---------------------------------------------------")
```

If you are running this on the local Db2 system, you do not need the PROTOCOL or the TCPIP parameter.

Summary

This appendix has presented the syntax with examples of almost all the ibm_db APIs. Feel free to use this chapter as a reference for writing your own Python programs.

Index

A

ACID test, 5
Atomicity, 5

B

backup command
    definition, 56
    import, 62
    syntax, 57, 58
    verification, 57
BACKUP DATABASE
        command, 57
Built-in functions (BIFs), 84
Business rules and constraints
    CHECK/Unique, 71
    DEFAULT, 72
    foreign keys, 70
    indexes, 69
    NOT NULL attribute, 67, 68
    primary key, 68, 69
    triggers, 72, 74, 75

C

Codd's paper, 1
Comma-separated
        values (CSV), 103
Consistency, 5
Constraints, 6

D

Databases
    activating, 36
    catalog views, 31
    connecting, 36
    creating, 34
    deactivating, 36
    definition, 30
    dropping, 36
    global configuration file, 33
    history files, 33
    listing, 35
    locking event monitor, 31
    logging files, 33
    objects, 30
    storage groups, 33
    tablespace, 32
Data Control Language (DCL), 6, 7
Data Definition Language (DDL), 6, 7
Data Manipulation Language (DQL), 7, 8
Data Query Language (DQL), 7
Db2
    development environment, 9, 10
    finished page, 18
    installation prerequisites, 10, 11
    installing, 12–14
    owner page, 15, 17, 18
    plan, 11, 12
    post0install, 19
    sample database, 20

211

© W. David Ashley 2021
W. D. Ashley, *Foundation Db2 and Python*, https://doi.org/10.1007/978-1-4842-6942-8

Printed in the United States
by Baker & Taylor Publisher Services

Printed in the United States
by Baker & Taylor Publisher Services